THE PERFECT TERM PAPER
Step by Step

Donald J. D. Mulkerne received his B.S. and Ed.M. degrees from Boston University and his Ed.D. from Columbia University. He has taught at Rockland (Massachusetts) High School, Catholic University of America, Boston University, Russell Sage College, College of St. Rose, and State University of New York at Albany (SUNYA).

He is the author of ten texts and reference books for high schools and colleges and more than twenty articles and research papers. Dr. Mulkerne has been the principal speaker at more than 150 high school commencement exercises, teachers' conventions, management conferences, and service club meetings. He conducts many workshops on written and oral communications.

Dr. Mulkerne has the rank of professor emeritus, SUNYA.

Donald J. D. Mulkerne, Jr., received his B.A. from Plattsburgh State University College (New York), his M.Ed. from Bowling Green State University (Ohio), and his Ph.D. from the University of Florida. He has been a counselor and teacher in the Bowling Green school system, Alachua County Public Schools (Florida), and was on the faculty at Sante Fe Community College (Florida).

Dr. Mulkerne is currently an Adjunct Associate Professor in the College of Medicine at the University of South Alabama, and is also in full-time practice as a counseling psychologist. He is the author of numerous articles and two books and is a frequent speaker at seminars, conventions, and professional meetings. He serves as a consultant to the Mobile County Sheriff's Department, the Albert Brewer Center, and Providence Hospital.

THE PERFECT TERM PAPER

Step by Step

DONALD J. D. MULKERNE, ED.D.
DONALD J. D. MULKERNE, JR., PH.D.

ANCHOR PRESS
Doubleday
NEW YORK
1988

Library of Congress Cataloging-in-Publication Data

Mulkerne, Donald J. D.
The perfect term paper.

Rev. ed. of: The term paper. 3rd rev. ed. 1983.
Includes index.
1. Report writing—Handbooks, manuals, etc.
2. Research—Handbooks, manuals, etc.
I. Mulkerne, Donald J. D., 1951–   .
II. Mulkerne, Donald J. D.   Term paper.   III. Title.
LB2369.M84   1987   808'.02   87-12630
ISBN 0-385-24794-X

CONTENTS

CONTENTS

THE PERFECT TERM PAPER
Step by Step

1

INTRODUCING THE TERM PAPER

THE PURPOSE OF THIS MANUAL

This book is designed to help you write your term paper—indeed, any research paper for which you must plan carefully to find, organize, and present information from a number of sources—whether this paper is your first or your twentieth.

It is a basic source of reference that will:

Help you choose a subject.

Show you how to get the most out of library resources.

Explain the purpose of the bibliography and footnotes as well as the mechanics of presenting them.

Suggest note-taking techniques.

Guide you in developing an outline.

Assist you in writing a paper from your outline so it will be prepared in acceptable style.

Show you how to set up simple tables.

Provide you with step-by-step procedures for preparing the finished typed copy of your paper.

Help you decide if you want the paper done on a word processor.

Include a finished term paper to illustrate the various procedures covered in this manual.

In addition to helping you write your term paper, Chapter 11 has a very complete listing of ideas on how to prepare and give an oral report based, perhaps, on sections of your term paper.

WHY WRITE TERM PAPERS?

Why do college students have to prepare term papers? Skills in English usage and experience in expressing ideas on paper in a readable and interesting manner can be acquired by writing original expository themes.

Preparing a term paper will:

Give you experience in locating information quickly and choosing among available sources as well as acquainting you with the library resources from which information can be drawn.

Teach you selectivity, for you will do much more reading than writing for your paper. You must not only choose from your reading what should be included in your paper, but also judge the relative importance of that information to your context.

Develop your writing skills and vocabulary so you can communicate more effectively.

In addition, writing a term paper is a valuable experience because it helps you to:

Think critically.

Become more knowledgeable about the topic you have researched.

Arrange your ideas in an orderly manner.

Write clearly, keeping in mind the reader's need to understand.

The preparation of a research paper, however, offers further challenges to you. It demands that you use your library skills to gather, interpret, and report on facts and ideas impartially, honestly, adequately, and clearly.

WHAT THE TERM PAPER IS NOT

The term paper is not a thesis or a dissertation. These two graduate papers go much more deeply into a particular subject and require a great deal of time, effort, research, and an extensive bibliography. In many cases, statistical interpretations are made. The term paper is less formal, shorter, shows evidence of some reading background, contains a bibliography, and often makes use of tables, graphs, and charts.

However, the term paper is not a popular novel. It should keep to facts, treat *pro* and *con* data fairly, and present its evidence in a scholarly manner that is interesting to read.

Neither is a term paper a mere listing of what several sources have to say about its topic. This kind of writing is lifeless, boring, and adds nothing to the knowledge already available on the subject. A worthwhile paper has form, its own introduction and conclusions.

Finally, a term paper is not:

A large number of footnotes designed only to impress the reader rather than to provide a means for in-depth reading about the topic or checking information contained in the paper.

A summary of one book or of what one person has to say about your topic.

A carelessly written composition containing many errors of grammar, logic, mechanics, and omissions of facts.

An attempt at original research of the laboratory-experimentation type commonly employed in doctoral dissertations.

WHAT THE TERM PAPER IS

Your term paper should be an unbiased account of a topic documented with pertinent, adequate, and valid information in support of whatever statements you make.

Your paper may be of the argumentative or of the storytelling type. The argumentative paper attempts to prove that something is right or wrong, good or bad, desirable or undesirable. The storytelling type surveys a subject by drawing upon pertinent references bearing upon a particular point, and then is written about the highlights of what has been read, without attempting to prove or disprove anything. The sample paper illustrated at the end of this manual is of the storytelling type. *(See Appendix B.)*

Documentation—the use of quotations—is a distinguishing feature of term papers. Each quotation has a footnote or endnote which identifies its source since it is important in this type of paper to know who said what. These quotations must be carefully selected and used only when really necessary to bring out a point you are trying to make. Too many quotations make for a choppy paper, and your instructor will note that he or she is reading what many other people think rather than what *you* think as illustrated by your choice of quotations. Failure to identify quoted matter and passing it off as one's own is *dishonest* and may well result in a failing mark. Do not plagiarize! Also considered dishonest is the practice of altering a previously written research paper or other printed matter by changing words, substituting different words, adding a sentence, or otherwise disguising the material so as to create the impression that it is of your own creation.

Purchasing a term paper from a research company is considered plagiarism and is dishonest. Buying a paper and submitting it as your own creation denies you the opportunity to learn how to write, how to express yourself, and how to do research.

The term paper, while its content is drawn from numerous sources, has the style of a well-written composition. Simply expressed, your paper will contain a short statement of its purpose, followed by your evidence presented in a logical manner and arranged for smooth reading. The paper will be completed with a few appropriate remarks which summarize the highlights of your research. Any conclusions you draw must be based upon your evidence. *(See sample Term Paper Pages 1 and 17 [purpose and conclusions].)*

Furthermore, the language of the paper will be related to its purpose. Are you trying to persuade, explain, relate, or entertain? Once you have decided this, you will know the degree of formality your paper should assume and the kind of vocabulary you should use. Using big words having many syllables without fully understanding their meaning may result in wrong word choices. Avoid trying to lengthen your paper by adding extra words just to reach a minimum set by your instructor. Conciseness, rather than wordiness, simplicity rather than floweriness, and clearness rather than abstruseness, should be your stylistic goals.

Finally, the term paper reflects you and the quality of your thinking. It should be factual and at the same time fair, including all evidence you find in your readings even though some of it may weaken your original position about your subject. Remember that progress is also made by discovering that what you once thought to be true is, in fact, false. What would you think of a pharmaceutical firm that put a drug on the market, guaranteed it to cure the common cold but failed to inform the public that severe headaches would result from its use? It is just as dishonest to mislead your reader by failing to include evidence contrary to your viewpoint and in so doing commit a serious error of omission. Such "slanting" is not likely to go unnoticed.

The most difficult job in writing is to get started. Begin where it is easiest for you: sit down and write all you now know about your subject—if you have one. If you have yet to select a subject, turn to Chapter 2. *See Nos. 8.6, 8.52.*

HOW IS THIS BOOK TO BE USED?

This manual provides key ideas to show you—as closely as any book can—exactly how to go about writing your paper. These key ideas are expressed in short simple sentences, each of which is numbered consecutively by chapter. Thus, beginning with Chapter 2, suggestions for writing an effective term paper appear as numbered items such as 2.1, 2.2, and so forth. In many instances, these numbers have been noted on the sample term paper at the end of the book. For example, look in Chapter 5 and locate 5.12. Read the item. Note that an example is provided in the term paper, page 6. Turn to that page in the term paper and you will find 5.12. This coding system enables you to easily look up the explanation or the reason for the use of a particular form.

Some users of this book prefer to read Chapter 1 and then go directly to the sample term paper and read it carefully, paying special attention to all items in boldface. Each of these refers them back to a particular chapter in the book. For example, 5.12 refers to Chapter 5, item 12 or 5.12. Then with that introduction of reading the term paper, they go back to Chapter 2 and proceed through the book systematically.

2

CHOOSING AND LIMITING THE SUBJECT

Choosing a subject is deceptively difficult and should not be treated lightly. While it may seem to require less physical effort than the other parts of preparing a paper, deciding on an appropriate subject and limiting it to a degree where you can give it the attention it needs will in the long run result in a completed paper of which you can be proud. Don't jump into choosing a topic. Selecting a topic impulsively or intuitively may cause you to regret your haste, for your paper may later bog down to a discouraging halt. Reflect upon each of the following suggestions, for they will help you get off to a good start.

2.1. Understand your assignment.

Listen to your instructor as he or she describes your term paper assignment. Understand its purpose, the length of the paper, the due date, the limits within which you must confine your subject, the type of paper you are to prepare—argumentative or narrative. Keep your instructor's comments on file and refer to them frequently.
See Nos. 2.5, 2.22, 7.2.

2.2. Your subject may be assigned, you may choose your own, or you may choose a subject within a certain area defined by your instructor.

If your instructor assigns you a subject, your task is simplified because you are now ready to make your plans for collecting the data. If you must choose your own subject, read items 2.3 through 2.21. If your subject must be confined within a certain area, such as English, History, or Geology, examine book and periodical indexes for ideas. Read Chapter 3 of this manual and then, if you have questions, consult with your college, school, or local librarian.

2.3. Think about your assignment, and if your instructor has invited discussion, go to him or her with your ideas.

Develop a tentative work plan by listing reference books, indexes, periodicals, and other aids which may be of assistance to you. Make a list of questions to ask your instructor. Write a thesis statement. Schedule an interview with your instructor and review these questions and your thesis statement with him or her.

See Nos. 2.1, 2.18, 2.22.

2.4. The title of your subject may be in the form of a question or a positive statement.

Subjects for term papers expressed in question form:

What Is the Process for Electing the President of the United States?

What Is the Value of Aerobic Exercise to Overweight Adults?

Does Noise in the Workplace Affect Worker Productivity?

Subjects of term papers expressed as statements:

The Election Process for the Office of President of the United States

The Value of Aerobic Exercise for Overweight Adults

Decreasing Noise in the Workplace to Improve Worker Productivity

2.5. Select a subject in line with the basic purposes of your course.

If you are completing a term paper for an English course, consider the advisability of writing about a subject in the English area. Determine the purpose of your term paper. Consider the reason that motivated your instructor to request such an assignment from you. As a result of writing your paper, are you supposed to be a better writer, a better thinker, a better researcher, or better informed about your subject? Knowing the reason for your assignment will help you write a paper in keeping with the requirements of your course.

See No. 2.1.

2.6. Select a subject in which you have a strong interest, curiosity, experience, or competency.

When interest and curiosity are present, your writing task becomes a delightful experience rather than a chore. Prior experience and competency in your subject reduce the danger of making unwise statements in your paper or failing to report the basic facts.

2.7. Select a subject in which information is readily available.

The subject should not be so new that information is difficult to obtain. Generally speaking, your school or college library or the local library should be well equipped, so that you can do all your reading in the local area. Consult your librarian and ask his or her opinion about the availability of data on your chosen subject. Choose a subject in which adequate and reliable information is available.

Examples of subjects having limited or unreliable data:
Alzheimer's Disease—Its Cause and Cure
U.S.A.—A.D. 3000
The Inside Story of Security Measures Taken at the John F. Kennedy Space Center
Booth's Private Conversations with His Conspirators
The Secret Thoughts of John Wilkes Booth
The Genealogy of the Conspirators of Lincoln

2.8. Select a subject with your audience in mind.

Be aware that another person will read your paper. If you know the viewpoint and the interest level of your instructor about your chosen subject, your paper will be more to the point and more interesting for him or her to read. If you know how informed your reader already is about your topic, it will be to your advantage to write a paper that goes beyond the reader's present range of knowledge. The reader should learn something by reading your paper.
See No. 11.20.

2.9. Select a subject important enough to warrant your attention, and if possible, one that correlates with other courses you are taking. In so doing you will then work with information that will help you improve in history or whatever.

Choose a subject that is intellectually respectable, offers practical value, and is capable of being developed fully into a thesis or a dissertation at some future time.

Examples of subjects lacking intellectual respectability or practical value:

Penguins of the South Pole (for a non-zoologist and a paper which has a travelogue flavor)

Fun at a Fair

The Manufacture of Christmas Candles

The Pizza Pie

2.10. Select a subject that can be researched within the time limits set by your instructor.

Determine how much time you have to complete your paper. Set deadlines for each phase of your research and writing task. Don't take on too ambitious a topic. Choose a broad subject area and then limit it.

Examples of subjects too ambitious for term papers:

Lincoln: The Full Story of the Assassination and Trial

The Rise and Fall of the Roman Empire

The Conquests of Napoleon

The World's Great Musicians

U.S. Presidents

The above topics might be used if they cover a smaller area.

Lincoln—His Final Days

The Rise of the Roman Empire

Napoleon Wins a Battle

American Composers of Jazz in the 1920s

U.S. Presidents of the Twentieth Century

2.11. Select a subject that is not too narrow.

Examples of subjects that are too narrow:

Hazardous Waste Damage in Lake Erie for January 1988

Diseases of Fleas

High School Economics for First-Semester Seniors in Alaska

Lincoln—His Service as a Postmaster

2.12. Select a subject that does not involve technical information beyond your comprehension.

Examples of subjects that might be too technical:

The Thermonuclear Bomb Ingredients

Drugs for Arthritis

Xerography—How It Works

Flights of Trajectories and Their Geometric Patterns

2.13. Select a subject suitable for student investigation and in good taste. A sensational subject appears more often to be a childish choice rather than a clever one. Someone is going to read your paper—make his or her time worthwhile.
  Examples of subjects not in good taste:
    The Heroic Qualities of Dillinger
    A Positive Look at Hedonism
    Earning a Living by Gambling

2.14. Select a subject that is not too neutral.
  Examples of subjects too neutral:
    Insurance Mortality Tables
    Filing Cases
    Advantages of Electricity over Gaslight

2.15. Select a subject that is clear.
  Examples of subjects that may not be clear:
    Quakers and Friends
    Running for the Office
    Banks

2.16. Select a subject that does not have a universal acceptance.
  Examples of subjects that have universal acceptance:
    Pollution Control Laws Are Needed
    AA—Does It Serve a Useful Purpose?
    Did John Wilkes Booth Kill Lincoln?

2.17. Select a topic that can be researched in your school, college, and/or local library. Therefore, before you commit yourself to a topic, be sure library references on this topic are available. If necessary, discuss your topic with a librarian to assess the availability of research data and library references.
  See No. 6.1.

2.18. After selecting a topic, write a thesis statement and your position or point of view about the subject you have chosen to research.
  See Nos. 2.19, 6.30.
  Example of topic:
    The Effects of Alcohol on Expectant Mothers
  Example of a thesis statement:
    The consumption of alcoholic beverages by expectant mothers, regardless of quantity, has been shown to have deleterious effects to both mother and fetus. The increase

in reported occurrences of Fetal Alcohol Syndrome (F.A.S.) in newborns is both alarming and epidemic in nature. This paper will explore the topic of alcohol use during pregnancy, and present facts supporting the argument that alcohol consumption by expectant mothers is unwise and potentially harmful to the baby.

2.19. The thesis statement suggests the direction you will take in developing your topic around one central theme. It also serves as a control device to keep you from straying off the topic no matter how tempting it may be to digress to interesting but irrelevant subtopics.

2.20. Choose from the following the most appropriate way of developing your paper:
A chronological approach
Comparing your topic with something else
Analyzing your topic by some method
Identifying problems and offering solutions
Giving your personal opinion but basing it on facts

2.21. If none of the suggestions in Nos. 2.3 to 2.17 help, and you are still searching for an idea for a paper, turn to Chapter 3 and pay particular attention to Nos. 3.44(a) to (v). An idea for a topic might come to mind merely by reading titles and content coverage of books and periodicals.

2.22. As you read this manual, you will see the need to have a conference with your instructor concerning your term paper assignment. During that conference, you might want to ask some of the following questions:

Chapter Reference	Question
2.2.	1. Will you assign me a topic or do I have free choice?
2.2. 2.5.	2. Must my topic be related to the content of this course?
2.3. 2.18. 2.19.	3. Should I develop a thesis statement, and do you want to see it?

5.5. 5.9. 5.36.	4. Do you wish me to use the traditional footnoting system or will endnotes be acceptable?
5.37. 5.41.	5. If I use endnotes, should they include both the content and referent type?
2.1. 8.1.	6. What is the due date for submitting the paper?
2.1. 8.2.	7. How long should the paper be? Number of pages, words, etc.?
9.19.	8. What is your preference about whether the paper should be single- or double-spaced?
9.20. 9.21. 9.22. 9.23.	9. What is your policy about correcting errors? For example, may I make pen-and-ink corrections, use some type of "cover-up," or retype the page?
9.38. 9.39.	10. Do you want my paper to have a title page?
Ch. 10 Intro.	11. Will you accept a paper done on a word processor?
Ch. 9. TYPING THE PAPER advice after 9.45.	12. Do you want my footnotes and bibliography done in single or double spacing?

Add your own questions here.

_____

_____

_____

_____

_____

_____

_____

3

USING THE LIBRARY

Libraries have become very sophisticated in recent years and have added many features and services to the science of storing and finding data and information. While most libraries still use the word *library* to identify their function, other terms may be used such as *Information Science Center* and *Information Resources Center.* The word *library* is used throughout this manual because it is the more common term.

The library is an educational tool. To get the greatest benefit from it, you must use it wisely. When you consider how often you will need the services of the library, you can appreciate the value of becoming skilled in library procedure. The benefits to be gained from wise use of the library facilities are numerous, but two override all others: pertinent references are easily located and time is saved when you "know your way around" in the library.

3.1. Most libraries prepare a set of instructions on how to use the facilities most effectively. Obtain a copy from the main desk or in the lobby and study it. Do this in advance of your actual research in the library.

3.2. Material found in the library usually is of three types:
general information
reference materials
periodicals

3.3. Most books "on reserve" must remain in the library during the day and are charged out only with permission at night, weekends, and holidays.

3.4. A Circulation or Loan Department charges out books (except those on reserve) for approximately two weeks.

3.5. Government publications and periodicals are usually not charged out but may be loaned for use in the Reading Room.

3.6. The Reference Librarian is a specialist in locating information and is available to help you when help is needed, or at any other time.

3.7. The Reference Room contains encyclopedias, handbooks, magazines, newspapers, and dictionaries of various types. Materials in this room are not available for overnight use.

3.8. The Periodicals Department is where you will find current newspapers and magazines. Usually, these materials are not available on a loan basis.

3.9. Many libraries have *divisional* reading rooms where books, periodicals, and other printed and audiovisual materials are gathered in special areas and grouped by subject matter. Such divisions often include Humanities, Social Studies, Sciences, Government Publications, Record Collection, and Newspapers. You may want to visit a *divisional* reading room to collect data for your paper.

3.10. An interlibrary loan service may be available whereby you may be able to borrow books, other printed matter, microfilms, and other audiovisuals for a modest charge. However, such service is usually slow—perhaps even weeks before you receive what you have requested. Allow enough time in your research plan in case you need to use this interlibrary loan service.

3.11. The library may have an Information Retrieval Section which can prepare computer-produced bibliographies using the ERIC, MEDLARS, *Psychological Abstracts,* and *Biological Abstracts* data bases. It may edit and distribute manually produced bibliographies and library guides.

3.12. Some university libraries are able to search by computer for information on many topics. References to journal articles, books, research reports, and other types of materials have been combined to form data bases, many of which correspond to printed indexes and abstracts covering a broad range of disciplines.

3.13. The result of a computer search is a bibliography or listing of citations to journal articles, serials, monographs, government publications, etc., related to your topic. Each citation includes full bibliographic information to help you locate items identified by the search. In some cases, abstracts or short summaries of the citations may also be printed if you request them. *Not all libraries are equipped to conduct computer searches.*

3.14. Consult your librarian to determine if a computer search is part of the library's service. If it is, the usual procedure is to complete a search request, defining your problem carefully in a concise narrative statement. Also, arrange for an appointment with the librarian who is trained to search the data base(s) you need. During your appointment, your request will be reviewed with you by the librarian, who, with your assistance, will formulate a search strategy.

3.15. (a) For example, ERIC is your major source for locating information on education topics. You need to become familiar with ERIC terminology in order to do your search. Using the *Thesaurus of ERIC Descriptors,* identify key descriptors (subject terms) relevant to your search, such as "Grading." You might also want to expand your search to include some of the narrower terms (NT), broader terms (BT), or related terms (RT) listed under the descriptor heading as shown in the example below.
See ERIC in Appendix D.

SN (scope note) denotes a term's usage in ERIC. UF (used for) is a cross-reference and should *not* be used for your search.

GRADING   **Jul. 1966**
CIJE: 716   RIE: 499
SN Process of rating an individual's or group's performance, achievement, or less frequently, behavior, using specifically established scales of values
UF Contract Grading #
Marking (Scholastic)
NT Credit No Credit Grading
Pass Fail Grading
BT Achievement Rating
RT Academic Achievement
Educational Testing
Grade Inflation

Grade Prediction
Grades (Scholastic)
Informal Assessment
Report Cards
Scoring
Student Evaluation
Student Teacher Relationship
Summative Evaluation

(b) Consult the monthly issues of *Resources in Education* (RIE). Check the Subject Index sections under the descriptor "Grading" and other applicable descriptors you have chosen to identify *titles* of current documents on the subject.

Check the semiannual and annual indexes to *Resources in Education* for relevant documents using the same descriptors.

Grade 8
Report on the Intermediate Evaluation Project.
                                           ED 164 622
Report on the Intermediate Evaluation Project-Phase II.
                                           ED 164 588

Grading
Institutional Research, Fiscal Year 1977: Perceptions of Mastery Grading. Research Monograph VIII.
                                           ED 164 061

Each document is identified by an accession number (ED plus six digits).

(c) Extend your search to the periodical literature by consulting the monthly indexes of *Current Index to Journals in Education* (CIJE).

Check the monthly, semiannual, and annual subject indexes of *Current Index to Journals in Education,* using the same descriptors.

Grading

A Contractual Examination: Another Alternative, *College English* v39 n3, pp368-70, Nov 77

EJ 169 448

"Sign Now, Pay Later": Further Experiments in Student Grading, *Exercise Exchange* v21 n1, pp9-12, F 76 EJ 169 477

Reporting Pupil Progress in Reading—Parents vs. Teachers, *Reading Teacher* v31 n3, pp294-6, Dec 77 EJ 169 510

Computer-Graded Homework in Introductory Physics, *American Journal of Physics* v45 n10, pp896-8, Oct 77 EJ 170 425

An Alternative Scoring Formula for Multiple-Choice and True-False Tests, *Journal of Educational Research* v70 n6, pp335-9, Jul/Aug 77 EJ 170 686

The identifying numbers for journal articles in CIJE are labeled EJ.

(d) From the Subject Indexes, go to the Document Résumé section of RIE or the Main Entry section of CIJE to read the abstract of the document or journal article. These sections are clearly marked, and the identifying numbers (ED or EJ) are listed consecutively. You can then determine whether you want to obtain the full text of the document or article. Availability information is given in each résumé.

EJ 169 477 CS 710 521
"Sign Now, Pay Later": Further Experiments in Student Grading Klein, Julie Thompson, *Exercise Exchange* v21 n1, pp9-12, F 76
*English Instruction, *Grading, *Teaching Techniques, *Contracts, Secondary Education, Higher Education
Presents an eight-point plan, with illustrations, for assigning student grades. (JM)
Reprint Available (See p. vii): UMI

Locate the journal articles (EJ accession numbers) in your library, or consult the introduction to CIJE for reprint ordering information.

(e) Notice how a full description of the title, source, publication date, number of pages, price, descriptors, and a summary of the research article is shown.

ED 164 061   JC 790 070
Institutional Research, Fiscal Year 1977: Perceptions
of Mastery Grading. Research Monograph VIII.
South Oklahoma City Junior Coll., Okla.
Pub Date—77
Note—53p.
EDRS Price MF-$0.83 HC-$3.50 Plus Postage.
Descriptors—*Academic Records, Administrator Attitudes, *Attitudes, Community Colleges, Counselor Attitudes, Employer Attitudes, Grades (Scholastic), *Grading, Higher Education, Institutional Research, *Junior Colleges, *Mastery Learning, School Funds, Secondary Education, Student Attitudes, Student Evaluation, Student Financial Aid, *Surveys, Teacher Attitudes, Transfer Policy, Transfer Students

The grading policy at South Oklahoma City Junior College (SOCJC) allows a student to master a course by doing a specified amount of work to a pre-determined standard (80% mastery). When this is accomplished, the student receives an "M" indicating mastery; otherwise, nothing appears on the official record. No A, B, C, grades are awarded. This document compiles six studies dealing with the perceptions of the "M" grade by different SOCJC constituencies. The first survey examined employers of the college's students. Employers preferred a traditional transcript though about two-thirds would accept a list of student competencies. Next studied were other institutions of higher education, which also preferred transcripts allowing student comparisons; however, no SOCJC students had been denied entrance to these transfer schools. A third study of financial aid offices examined effects on both student aid at transfer institutions as well as on SOCJC's ability to obtain student aid funds. It appeared students may have had trouble getting scholarships, though the college itself had no problem getting funds. A need was seen for added information and explanation about the system in the next survey of high school counselors. The fifth survey concerned student attitudes. About 40-45% saw the "M" as an advantage, while 23-30% saw it as a disadvantage. The final report studied faculty and staff perceptions. The majority felt the system was an advantage to students but the problems in transferring and the fact that there is no reward for excellence were disadvantages. (MB)

3.16. The Microfilm Department, if your library has one, has reduced thousands of printed and written matter to microscopic size. Film copies of the New York *Times* and other major newspapers are usually available for viewing on special machines that magnify the print.

Microcard, microcopy, microfiche, microfilm, and microprint refer to the manner in which data are stored. The generic word for this is *microform* which is a process of reproducing printed and written matter in a much-reduced size. Some type of film reader is required. A Microform Room stores newspapers, periodicals, and books on microfilm, microfiche, and microcards.

While only the most modern libraries have all this equipment, there is a good chance that *some* of it is available. Check with the librarian.

3.17. Automation is becoming more and more important and visible in library services. Long Distance Xerography (referred to as LDX) where available, allows you to get Xerox copies of printed matter in minutes. However, this service is currently available only to librarians rather than to library users.

3.18. Many libraries have copying machines. A modest fee is charged for their use. Rather than hand-copying a page from a book, you might want to make a Xerox copy of it as this will save you writing time. A microprinter may also be available.

3.19. Librarians are available to answer intelligent questions—even questions that are not clearly thought out. Understand clearly the nature of your problem before asking for help. But if you need help, your librarian is waiting to assist you.

3.20. If you have a "dial access" system in the library, you may be able to get special and unusual help from a master computer console. This console stores great quantities of data and information. Ask your librarian for help.

3.21. Many librarians have audiovisual equipment available for use in the library including movie projectors, overhead projectors, tape recorders, record players, slide and filmstrip projectors. A Learning Resources Center, if one is available, usually includes the Curriculum Library Collection, non-print media, and the phonograph record collection. Record players and earphones are usually available.

3.22. If the library is equipped with electronic carrels, ask your librarian for assistance. Typical carrels are equipped with TV, earphones, radios, motion picture projectors, and screen, slide viewers, typewriters, and other A-V aids.

3.23. If the library has a Special Collections Section, it will probably contain materials that require special treatment such as manuscripts, rare books, reprint series, and specialized subject collections.

3.24. Rotary files have inserts with typed or printed headings listing the periodicals subscribed to and available in the Periodical Room.

3.25. Some libraries have moved away from having a card catalog to a computer printout and/or terminal where all books, periodicals, and other matter in that particular library are listed.

3.26. Use 3-inch by 5-inch white lined cards to record your notes as you gather data for your paper. Hold the cards horizontally and write on the lines.

3.27. Do some preliminary research to be sure you can locate information and data easily on your chosen subject. Proceed as follows:

Develop a preliminary bibliography, placing one reference only on each of your cards. These references relate to the subject you will develop in your paper. One of the following general references may give you an overview of your subject as a basis for further development:*

---

* *A, An,* and *The* appearing as the first word in a title of a general reference are generally ignored in alphabetizing those references. The first letter of the next word determines the alphabetical order.

> *Academic American Encyclopedia*
> *Collier's Encyclopedia*
> *Encyclopedia Americana*
> *Encyclopaedia Britannica*
> *Funk & Wagnalls New Encyclopedia*
> *Harper World Encyclopedia*
> *New American Encyclopedia*
> *New Caxton Encyclopedia*
> *New Columbia Encyclopedia*
> *New Lincoln Library Encyclopedia*
> *New Standard Dictionary*
> *Pears Cyclopaedia*
> *Random House Encyclopedia*
> *University Desk Encyclopedia*
> *Volume Library*
> *World Book Encyclopedia*

3.28. Other sources in the library that will help you locate information include the following tools:
card catalog, periodical indexes, rotary files, vertical files, or all three. See Nos. 3.31–.34, 3.38 for examples of the card catalog and periodical index. Vertical files are file cases in which are stored various and sundry matter such as booklets and catalogs received by the library. Consult the *Vertical File Index* for a listing of such material from 1935.

3.29. The card catalog generally lists books and periodicals that are bound. Some libraries list audiovisual materials except films. The card catalog is made up of 3-inch by 5-inch unlined white cards either in type or print listing all books, reference books, and other contents of the library.
See Nos. 3.31 and 3.32.

3.30. The card catalog lists each book three ways:
author, title, and subject
See No. 3.31.

3.31. The card catalog includes typed cards prepared by the local library.

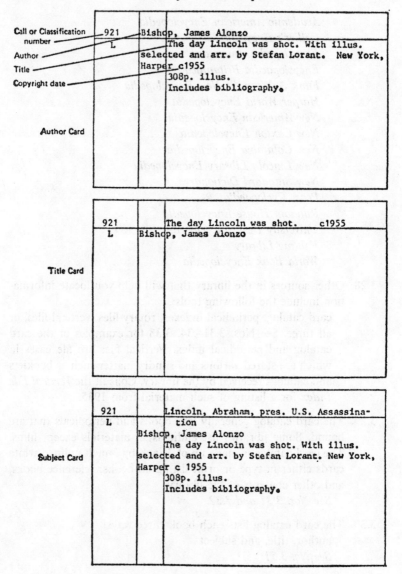

Call or Classification number
Author
Title
Copyright date

921
L
Bishop, James Alonzo
The day Lincoln was shot. With illus.
selected and arr. by Stefan Lorant. New York,
Harper c1955
  308p. illus.
  Includes bibliography.

Author Card

921
L
The day Lincoln was shot.   c1955
Bishop, James Alonzo

Title Card

921
L
Lincoln, Abraham, pres. U.S. Assassina-
  tion
Bishop, James Alonzo
The day Lincoln was shot. With illus.
selected and arr. by Stefan Lorant. New York,
Harper c 1955
  308p. illus.
  Includes bibliography.

Subject Card

3.32. The card catalog also has printed cards obtained from the Library of Congress. These cards provide the same general information as the local library cards shown in No. 3.31.

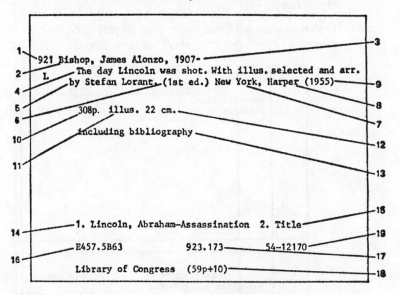

1 Call or Classification No.
2 Author
3 Date of birth of author
4 Title of book
5 Name of illustrator
6 Edition
7 Place of publication
8 Publisher
9 Copyright date
10 No. of pages in book

11 Book is illustrated
12 Size of type
13 Book has bibliography
14 Information for librarian
15 Information for librarian
16 Library of Congress Catalog no.
17 Dewey Decimal Classification no.
18 Library of Congress information
19 Card order no.

3.33. If several books are listed for the same author and have the same title, examine the most recent one first, as it is assumed to be the most nearly correct and up-to-date in its treatment of the subject matter.

3.34. If references are not listed under your subject title, you may be referred by "See" and "See also" cards to similar topics.

		Manslaughter	see
		Assassination Homicide Murder	

"See" Card

		Assassination	see also
		Anarchism and anarchists Murder Regicides Terrorism.	

"See also" Card

3.35. All books have author, subject, and title cards. For some books, such as a collection of poems or biographies, another type of card may be prepared, known as an analytic card. This card serves to call your attention to a small portion of another book which carries information on your subject.

For example, if you wished to write a term paper on the assassination of Abraham Lincoln, you might note the following reference on an analytic card if you were to check the card catalog under Lincoln:

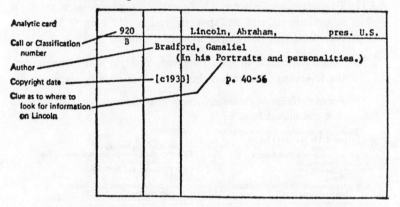

Analytic card

Call or Classification number

Author

Copyright date

Clue as to where to look for information on Lincoln

920
B
Lincoln, Abraham,   pres. U.S.
Bradford, Gamaliel
(In his Portraits and personalities.)
[c1931]   p. 40-56

3.36. (a) The Dewey Decimal System classifies books numerically:

000 General Works
100 Philosophy and Related Disciplines
200 Religion
300 The Social Sciences
400 Language

500 Pure Science
600 Technology (Applied Science)
700 The Arts
800 Literature and Rhetoric
900 General Geography and History

Note that the call or classification number of the book shown on the analytic card above is 920. Also note that the Dewey Decimal System reserves the 900 section for books on history.

(b) The Library of Congress System (often used in large university libraries) classifies books according to the alphabet:

A   General Works, Polygraphy, and Bibliography
B   Philosophy, Psychology, and Religion

C   Auxiliary Sciences of History
D   General and Old World History (except America)
E–F   American History

G	Geography, Anthropology, Manners and Customs, Folklore, Recreation	Q	Science
		R	Medicine
		S	Agriculture, Plant and Animal Industry, Fish Culture, and Fisheries, Hunting Sports
H	Social Science		
J	Political Science		
KF	Law of the United States		
L	Education	T	Technology
M	Music and Books on Music	U	Military Science
		V	Naval Science
N	Fine Arts	Z	Bibliography and Library Science
P	Language and Literature		

3.37. To ascertain whether any information on your topic is available in periodicals and newspapers, you would consult the many periodical and newspaper indexes available.

3.38. While periodical indexes may vary in style and arrangement, the following illustration shows the data usually given:

Readers' Guide to Periodical Literature. [1] General periodicals by author and subject from 1900.

Education in cooperation: new ventures reported. Lib J 100:1763 0 1 '75
  See also
Library institutes and workshops
1 — LIBRARY science
  — *See also*
Cataloging
LIBRARY seminars. See Library institutes and workshops
LIBRARY standards. See College libraries—Standards
LIBRARY workshops. See Library institutes and workshops
LIBYA
  Expropriation policy
Blows at Hammer; Occidental petroleum's subsidiary. por Time 106:62 0 13 '75
  Politics and government
Why Kaddafi piped down. B. Came. por Newsweek 86:36+ S 22 '75
LICENSES
  See also
Radio operators, Amateur—Licenses
LIDS, Canning jar. See Canning and preserving
2 —   —Equipment and supplies
LIE detectors and detection
Right way to use a lie detector. D. T. Lykken. il por Psychol Today 8:56-60+ bibl (p98) Mr '75: Discussion. 9-12-13 Ag '75
3 — Yes to lie detector tests for private employees; il Nations Bus 63:16 Ag '75

LIGHTNING
  See also
Golf—Lightning hazards
LIGHTNING suppression (weather control) See Weather control
LIGHTS, Traffic. See Traffic signals
LILIES
Lilies are for everyone. E. A. McRae. fl Horticulture 53:26-8+ S '75 — 4
LIMBS, Artificial
  See also
Hands, Artificial
LIMITATION OF ACTIONS
Statutes of limitation: an overview. A. T. Kornblut. Archlr Rec 158:49-50 Ag '75 — 5
LIN, C. C. and Van De Sande, J. H.
Differential fluorescent staining of human chromosomes with daunomycin and adriamycin—the D-bands. bibl il Science 190: 61-3 0 3 '75 — 6 / 7
LINCOLN, Abraham — 8
  Addresses, messages, etc.
Reflections—the Gettysburg address. M. J. Adler and W. Gorman. New Yorker 51:42-4+ S 8 '75 — 9 / 10
  Assassination
True history of the assassination of Abraham Lincoln and the conspiracy of 1865. by b. — 11
Weichmann. Review
  New Repub +73-91+2 S 20 '75. S. F. — 12
Lee — 13

1 "See" and "See also" references
2 Article contains bibliography
3 Article is illustrated
4 Volume number of periodical
5 Date of periodical
6 Page number of periodical
7 Main heading
8 Subheading
9 Title of article
10 Article is continued in back of periodical
11 Review of book
12 Name of periodical
13 Author of article

[1] *Readers' Guide to Periodical Literature* Copyright © 1975 by The H. W. Wilson Company. Material reproduced by permission of the publisher.

3.39. *The Nineteenth Century Readers' Guide to Periodical Literature, 1890–99,* includes author, subject, and illustrator entries for short stories, novels, plays, and poems. Book reviews are also indexed.

3.40. Book indexes usually list most books published. These indexes are arranged by author, subject, and title. This index differs from the library card catalog which lists only books found in that particular library.

3.41. General periodical indexes are excellent starting points for locating information not generally found in books. The more common indexes are:

Christian Science Monitor Index, from 1960
Directory of Newspapers and Periodicals, from 1880
New York Times Index, from 1913
Poole's Index to Periodical Literature, 1802–1907
Readers' Guide to Periodical Literature, from 1900
Times Index, from 1906

3.42. *Guide to Reference Books* lists reference books basic to research. General and specific books and other printed matter are listed. It is extremely helpful in making a systematic study of reference books available, classified by subject matter.

3.43. In addition to the above, No. 3.42, you should consult *Introduction to Reference Work* by Katz (McGraw-Hill Book Company). Volume I provides basic information sources, and Volume II explains the various reference services available in the library.

3.44. Another important source for gathering information for your paper is to refer to specialized reference books. The following list, arranged by subject matter, should help you get started:

(a) Accounting, Banking, Business, Economics, Finance
Accountants Digest, from 1935. Subject index.
Applied Science and Technology Index, from 1958. Subject index.
Business Information: How to Find and Use It
Business Periodicals Index, from 1958. Accounting, advertising, automation, banking, finance, general business, insurance, labor and management, taxa-

tion, transportation, specific businesses, industries, trade. Subject index.

Commercial Atlas and Marketing Guide

Dictionary of Data Processing

Dictionary of Economics

Encyclopedia of Accounting Systems

Encyclopedia of Banking and Finance

Encyclopedia of Management

Encyclopedic Dictionary of Systems and Procedures

Financial Handbook

How to Use the Business Library

Industrial Arts Index, 1913–57. Changed to *Applied Science and Technology Index,* and *Business Periodicals Index* in 1958.

Insurance Periodical Index

Journal of Economic Literature

Predicast's F&S Index United States

Wall Street Journal Index, from 1957

(b) Agriculture, Biology, Chemistry, Medicine

Agriculture Engineer's Handbook, from 1961

Applied Science and Technology Index, from 1958. Geology, metallurgy, physics. Subject index. Formerly, *Industrial Arts Index.*

Bibliography of the History of Medicine

Biological Abstracts, from 1926

Biological and Agricultural Index, from 1964. Agriculture, biology, forestry, home economics, veterinary medicine. Subject index. Until 1964, listed as *Agricultural Index.*

Biology and Medicine

Biology Data Book

Blakiston's New Gould Medical Dictionary

Chemical Abstracts, from 1907

Cumulated Index Medicus, from 1960. Author and subject index.

Current List of Medical Literature, from 1941

Drug Interaction: An Annotated Bibliography with Selected Excerpts, 1967–70

Encyclopedia of Chemistry

Encyclopedia of Food

Environmental Abstracts, 1971–73
Grzimek's Animal Life Encyclopedia
Handbook of Biochemistry and Molecular Biology
Handbook of Chemistry and Physics
Index Medicus, 1879–1927. Author and subject index.
Taber's Cyclopedic Medical Dictionary

(c) Anthropology

Abstracts in Anthropology
Abstracts of Folklore Studies
American Negro Reference Book
Dictionary of Anthropology
Harvard Encyclopedia of American Ethnic Groups
International Bibliography of Social and Cultural Anthropology
The Negro Almanac
Peoples of All Nations
A Study in Race & Culture Contacts
When Peoples Meet

(d) Art, Music

Art Index, from 1929. Archaeology, architecture, arts and crafts, ceramics, decoration and ornament graphic arts, industrial design, interior decoration, landscape architecture, painting, sculpture. Author and subject index.
Catalog of Museum Publications and Media, from 1980
Complete Opera Book
Dictionary of Modern Sculpture
Dictionary of Musical Terms
Encyclopedia of the Arts
Encylopedia of World Art
Guide to Art Reference Books
Guide to the Performing Arts, from 1957
Harvard Dictionary of Music
Music Index, from 1949. Author and subject index.
New Grove Dictionary of Music and Musicians
The New Kobbé's Complete Opera Book
The Oxford Companion to Art
A Standard History of Music

(e) Biography

American Men and Women of Science

Appleton's Cyclopedia of American Biography
Biography Index, from 1947. Indexed by profession and occupation.
Chambers's Biographical Dictionary
Contemporary Authors
Current Biography Yearbook, from 1940
Dictionary of American Biography, 1928–37. Important people in American history no longer living.
Dictionary of American Scholars; a biographical directory
Dictionary of International Biography
Dictionary of National Biography, 1882–1967. Important people in English history.
The International Who's Who
Leaders in Education
McGraw-Hill Encyclopedia of World Biography
Webster's American Biographies
Webster's Biographical Dictionary
Who Was Who in America
Who's Who, from 1948. Important living English persons.
Who's Who in America, from 1899
Who's Who in American Education
Who's Who in the East
The Writer's Directory

(f) Education

American Library Directory
Bibliographic Guide to Educational Research
Business Education Index
Canadian Education Index
Current Index to Journals in Education (CIJE)
Dictionary of Education
Dissertation Abstracts International
Education Abstracts, 1949–65
Educational Administration Abstracts
Education Index, from 1929. Child study, comparative education, curriculum development, educational psychology, educational research, elementary education, higher education, school administration, sec-

ondary education, statistical methods, teacher education, and related subjects. Subject index.

Educational Resources Information Center (ERIC)
Encyclopedia of Education
Encyclopedia of Educational Research
How to Locate Educational Information and Data
Research in Education (ERIC), from 1966
Resources in Education/ERIC
Review of Educational Research
Statistical Yearbook, from 1963
Thesaurus of ERIC Descriptors

(g) Energy and the Environment

The Energy Index
The Environmental Index
International Aerospace Abstracts
Nuclear Science Abstracts
Oceanic Abstracts, from 1978
Pollution Abstracts, from 1971

(h) Engineering, Science, Technology

Abstracts & Indexes in Science & Technology: A Descriptive Guide
Aerospace Yearbook
American Men and Women of Science
Applied Science and Technology Index, from 1958. Aeronautics, automation, chemistry, construction, electricity, electrical communication, engineering, geology, metallury, industrial and related subjects. Replaces the *Industrial Arts Index*.
Engineer's Year-Book, from 1894
A Guide to Information in Space Science and Technology
Industrial Arts Index, 1913–57. Engineering, trade, business. Ceased publication in 1957; replaced by *Applied Science and Technology Index* and the *Business Periodicals Index*. Subject index.
International Aerospace Abstracts, from 1961
McGraw-Hill Encyclopedia of Science and Technology
Nuclear Science Abstracts, from 1948
Sources of Engineering Information
Van Nostrand's Scientific Encyclopedia

(i)   Geology, Geography
        Aids to Geographical Research
        Annotated Bibliography of Economic Geology
        *Bibliography and Index of Geology Exclusive of North
            America,* from 1934. Subject index.
        Bibliography of North American Geology
        Encyclopedia of World Regional Geology, from 1975
        Geological Abstracts
        Geological Dictionary
        Guide to Geologic Literature
        Social Sciences and Humanities Index, from 1916. For-
            merly *International Index.* Author and subject in-
            dex.
        Webster's New Geographical Dictionary
(j)   History
        America: History and Life
        American Historical Documents
        The Beards' New Basic History of the United States
        Current Digest of the Soviet Press
        Dictionary of American History
        Dictionary of Dates
        Encyclopedia of American History
        An Encyclopedia of World History
        Guide to Historical Literature
        Guide to Historical Reading
        Harvard Guide to American History
        Historical Abstracts
        Historical Atlas
        Webster's Guide to American History
(k)   Language, Acronyms, Synonyms, Proverbs, Quotations
        Acronyms, Initialisms, and Abbreviations Dictionary
        Allen's Synonyms and Antonyms
        Dictionary of Acronyms and Abbreviations
        *Dictionary of American Proverbs and Proverbial
            Phrases, 1820–80*
        Dictionary of American Slang
        Dictionary of Contemporary American Usage
        Early American Proverbs & Proverbial Phrases
        Familiar Quotations by Bartlett
        FPA Book of Quotations

The Home Book of Bible Quotations
Hoyt's New Cyclopedia of Practical Quotations
Language and Language Behavioral Abstracts
The Modern Dictionary of Quotations
Oxford Dictionary of Quotations
The Quotation Dictionary
Quotations for All Occasions
Quotations for Speakers
Racial Proverbs
Roget's International Thesaurus
Roget's Thesaurus of Synonyms and Antonyms
Speech Index, 1935–61. Author, subject and type of
    speech index.
Standard Handbook of Synonyms, Antonyms, and
    Prepositions
Stevenson's Home Book of Quotations
Webster's New Dictionary of Synonyms

(l) Literature
Articles on American Literature, 1900–1950
Book Review Digest, from 1905
Book Review Index
Cambridge History of American Literature
Cassell's Encyclopedia of World Literature
Contemporary Literary Criticism
Essay and General Literature Index
A Glossary of Literary Terms
Granger's Index to Poetry
Guide to American Literature and Its Background,
    since 1890
McGraw-Hill Encyclopedia of World Drama
The Oxford Companion to American Literature
Play Index
The Reader's Companion to World Literature
The Reader's Encyclopedia
Short Story Index

(m) Mathematics, Physics
CRC Handbook of Mathematical Sciences
Encyclopedia of Computer Sciences and Technology
Encyclopedic Dictionary of Mathematics
Guide to the Literature of Mathematics and Physics

Handbook of Chemistry and Physics
Mathematics Dictionary
Physics Abstracts
World of Mathematics

(n)   Mythology, Folklore

A Bibliography of North American Folklore and Folksong
Abstracts of Folklore Studies
Folklore Index
Folklore of the American Negro Mythologies
Folksong Style & Culture
Mythology of All Races
Religions, Mythologies, Folklore
Religions of the World
Treasury of American Folklore
A Treasury of American Superstitions

(o)   Nations, Political Science

A Guide to the Use of United States Documents
Handbook of Latin American Studies
Index to Latin American Periodical Literature, 1929–60. Economics, politics, government. Author and subject index.
International Bibliography of Political Science
International Political Science Abstracts
Public Affairs Information Service Bulletin (PAIS), from 1915
Worldmark Encyclopedia of the Nations

(p)   Philosophy

Bibliography of Philosophical Bibliographies
Dictionary of Philosophy and Psychology
Encyclopedia of Philosophy
Handbook in the History of Philosophy

(q)   Psychology

American Men and Women of Science
Dictionary of Behavioral Science
Dictionary of Philosophy and Psychology
Dictionary of Psychology
Encyclopedia of Psychology
Encyclopedia of Sexual Behavior
Harvard List of Books in Psychology

Psychological Abstracts, from 1927
Psychological Index, 1895–1931. Author index.
Thesaurus of Psychological Index Terms
(r)   Radio, Television
Educational Media Index, 1964. Master title index.
Encyclopedic Dictionary of Electronics and Nuclear Engineering
Guides to Newer Educational Media
International Television Almanac, from 1956
Radio Amateur's Handbook
Radio-Television-Electronic Dictionary
Sources of Information on Educational Media
Television Almanac
Television Manual
What's the Right Word?
(s)   Recreation, Sports
Bibliography of Swimming
The Dictionary of Sports
Early American Sports
Encyclopedia of Sports
How-to-Do-It Book
Hunter's Encyclopedia
Index to Handicrafts, Model-making, and Workshop Projects. Subject index.
Official Encyclopedia of Baseball
Traditional Games of England, Scotland, and Ireland
(t)   Religion
The American Book of Days
Catholic Periodical and Literature Index, from 1930
Dictionary of the Bible
Encyclopedia Judaica
Encyclopedia of Religion and Ethics
A Guide to American Catholic History
The Home Book of Bible Quotations
Index to Jewish Periodicals, from 1963. Selected American and Anglo-Jewish journals. Author and subject index.
Index to Religious Periodical Literature, from 1960. Basically Protestant with some Jewish and Roman Catholic listings. Author and subject index.

Jewish Encyclopedia
New Catholic Encyclopedia
Religions, Mythologies, Folklore

(u)   Social Science
Abstracts for Social Workers
Abstracts on Criminology and Penology
British Humanities Index
Crime and Delinquency Abstracts
Criminology Index (1945–72)
Current Contents: Social and Behavioral Sciences
Demographic Yearbook
Dissertational Abstracts International
Encyclopedia of Social Work
Encyclopedia of the Social Sciences
A Guide to Periodical Literature in the Social Sciences and the Humanities, 1955–65. Renamed *Social Sciences Citation Index*, from 1973
Humanities Index, from 1974. Supersedes in part *Social Sciences and Humanities Index*. Archaeology, classics, folklore, history, language, literature, performing arts, philosophy, religion, and related subjects. Author and subject index.
Human Resources Index
International Encyclopedia of the Social Sciences
International Index, 1907–52. Renamed *Social Sciences Index*, 1953–64. Renamed *Social Sciences and Humanities Index*, from 1966. Author and subject index.
Psychological Abstracts
Public Affairs Information Service Bulletin (PAIS), from 1915
Readers' Guide to Periodical Literature
Social Sciences and Humanities Index
Social Sciences Citation Index
Sources of Information in the Social Sciences
Women's Studies Abstracts

(v)   United States, Public Documents
The Book of the States, from 1935
Dictionary of American History, 1940–44
Documents of American History, 1962

> *Monthly Catalog of United States Government Publications,* from 1895
> *Official Congressional Record*
> *A Popular Guide to Government Publications,* 1951–62. Subject index.
> *Public Affairs Information Service Bulletin* (PAIS)
> *Readex Microprint,* from 1953. Author and subject index.
> *Statistical Abstract of the United States,* from 1878

3.45. Almanacs, and general yearbooks, provide valuable information for developing a paper. Some of the more important ones are listed below:

> *Americana Annual,* from 1923
> *American Yearbook,* from 1910
> *Collier's Encyclopedia Year Book,* from 1939
> *Demographic Yearbook,* from 1948
> *Economic Almanac,* from 1940
> *Facts on File, Weekly News Digest with Cumulative Index,* from 1940
> *Guinness Book of World Records,* from 1964
> *Information Please Almanac,* from 1947
> *Public Affairs Information Service Bulletin* (PAIS), from 1915
> *Reader's Digest Almanac*
> *Statesman's Year-book,* from 1864
> *Statistical Abstract of the United States,* from 1878
> *Whitaker's Almanack,* from 1869 (British)
> *World Almanac and Book of Facts,* from 1868
> *World Book Year Book,* from 1962
> *Yearbook of Agriculture,* from 1894
> *Yearbook of the United Nations,* from 1946

3.46. Atlases contain maps and economic information. Some of the most recent include:

> *Encyclopaedia Britannica World Atlas*
> *Goode's World Atlas*
> *Oxford World Atlas*
> *Rand McNally Commercial Atlas and Marketing Guide*
> *Rand McNally New Cosmopolitan World Atlas*
> *Rand McNally Premier World Atlas*

3.47. Word dictionaries are essential for developing a paper. The following dictionaries are up to date and extremely helpful:

The American Heritage Dictionary
Funk & Wagnall's New Standard Dictionary
The Oxford English Dictionary
Random House Dictionary of the English Language
Thorndike Barnhardt Dictionary
Webster's New Collegiate Dictionary
Webster's New International Dictionary
Webster's Third New International Dictionary

Italian, French, German, Russian, and Spanish dictionaries are also in print.

3.48. Microforms have added tremendously to the storehouse of knowledge contained in the library and offer great promise for providing information for your paper. You will need the librarian's help to locate:

Guide to Microforms in Print
Newspapers on Microfilm
Readex Microprint
Subject Guide to Microforms in Print
Union List of Microforms
A Union List of Publications in Opaque Microforms

3.49. To determine if a particular book is in print, consult:

Book Review Digest, from 1905. "See" and "See also" references included.

Books in Print, from 1948. Author and subject index.

Cumulative Book Index, from 1929. Monthly supplements to the *United States Catalogue.* Includes all books published in the United States except textbooks and also includes books published and printed in the English language anywhere in the world. Listed by author, subject, and title. Useful in reading about a subject when the book is not found in the local library.

Paperbound Books in Print, from 1955. Author and subject index.

United States Catalog: Books in Print

United States Catalogue, from 1928. Books published in the United States on a particular subject.

3.50. Many libraries have special facilities for disabled library users and their aides. Most libraries will have books in large type and Braille or other special formats. A modern library or a university-affiliated library may have specialized equipment, such as Kurtzwell Reading Machine, Opticon, Braille typewriter, magnifying glasses, talking book players, automatic page-turners, computer-assisted reading aids, and other technologically advanced equipment that some public libraries cannot afford. Other types of special services, such as interlibrary loans, books-by-mail, and xerography (copiers) are available by telephone at many libraries. Inquire of the Coordinator of Library Services for the Disabled or of a librarian of the services available, if you require assistance.

4

PREPARING THE BIBLIOGRAPHY
AND FOOTNOTES

Do not become overwhelmed by the abundance of material that may be available on your subject. Select your bibliography with care, so that it is not cluttered with references of little, if any, value to you. Spend considerable time on this bibliography because it will pay you dividends, not only in the opportunity it provides you to broaden your understanding and knowledge of your subject but also in the clues and ideas it offers which will help you develop your paper.

4.1. A working bibliography is a list of the sources of information selected by you.
    See No. 9.136.

4.2. The final bibliography appears at the end of the term paper and lists only those references that you use from your working bibliography.

4.3. Each reference in your working bibliography is recorded in ink on separate 3 by 5 cards.

Author's name
Title of Reference
Facts of Reference
Edition
Volume number
Place of publication
Name of publisher
Date of publication
Comments (optional)

Current, Richard N.
Mr. Lincoln
N.Y.: Dodd, Mead and Co.
1957
[see page 382 - Lincoln expresses his feelings about his own safety against would-be assassins.]

4.4. A typical term paper usually requires as many as 50 bibliographic references even though all are not included in the writing of the paper.

4.5. As you prepare your working bibliography, you will constantly be adding new cards and eliminating others.

4.6. By pruning, screening, adding, and deleting cards, your working bibliography develops into your final bibliography, which is a selected list of references far fewer in number than you originally had.
    See No. 9.136.

4.7. Examine appropriate books for information on your subject, quickly checking the table of contents, chapter headings, and index. Check for a bibliography at ends of chapters and at the end of the book.

4.8. After completing your first bibliography, prune or screen it by removing and placing in a separate pack the references that hold little promise of information about your subject. Save all cards in case you need the references later.

4.9. If a book reference holds promise, go to the card catalog and write the classification number in the upper left-hand corner of your 5 by 3 card.
    See Nos. 3.31–.32.

4.10. If a periodical reference holds promise for you, check with your librarian to see if the library carries that particular magazine or newspaper.
    NOTE: You will see that certain abbreviations and foreign expressions customarily appear in *italics,* both in this book and in your reading. Whenever you include such words in a paper, they should be underlined.

4.11. A proper form for footnotes (F) and their bibliographic partners (B) appears in Nos. 4.12–.49.
    Here are the component parts of each:
    Footnote:
    Author's name (in signature order)
    Title of reference
    Volume number (if applicable)

Publication place
Publisher
Date of publication
Page reference
See No. 5.4.
Bibliography:
Author's name (last name first)
Title of reference
Volume number (if applicable)
Place of publication
Publisher
Date of publication

As you examine the footnote at No. 4.12 F, notice how the first line is indented seven spaces; second line in footnote is flush (begins) at the left margin. Footnote No. 4.12 does not have a volume number but notice No. 4.21 F.

The reverse is true when typing the bibliography. Notice No. 4.12 B. The first line begins at the left margin. Second line is indented seven spaces. See No. 4.21 B and notice where the volume number is located.

The mechanics of typing a bibliography and footnotes in correct form are deceivingly simple. However, many entrapments await the person who is careless about underlining, quotation marks, commas, periods, parentheses, and other considerations required for correctly typing footnotes and a bibliography.

A research paper requires documentation if it is to be of value both to the writer and to the reader. This documentation, while it may be a necessary evil, *is* necessary. Why? A good researcher must be able to retrace the steps taken to verify, for example. Therefore, your bibliography and footnotes must be both complete and accurate.

This section of Chapter 4 lists the kinds of references you commonly encounter in doing research on a term paper. Because you will be placing your footnotes at the bottom of the page and the bibliography at the end of the paper, the listing is arranged in the order you see it. The footnote (F) is shown and is followed by the form used when the footnote becomes part of the bibliography (B). Of course, the F and B are used here only to identify what you are looking at—a footnote and its bibliographic partner.

```
4.12. BOOK--Anonymous works
   F        Textbooks Are Indispensable! (New York: The
   American Textbook Publishers Institute, [n.d.]), p. 32.
```

B   <u>Textbooks Are Indispensable!</u> New York: The American Textbook Publishers Institute [n.d.].

4.13. BOOK--One author

F   William F. Buckley, Jr. <u>Atlantic High</u> (Garden City, NY: Doubleday & Company, Inc., 1982), p. 41.

B   Buckley, William F., Jr. <u>Atlantic High</u>. Garden City, NY: Doubleday & Company, Inc., 1982.

4.14. BOOK--Two authors

F   Carl Graver and Linda Morse, <u>Helping Children of Divorce: A Group Leader's Guide</u> (Springfield, IL: Charles C. Thomas, 1986), p. 46.

B   Graver, C. M. and Morse, L. M. <u>Helping Children of Divorce: A Group Leader's Guide</u>. Springfield, IL: Charles C. Thomas, 1986.

4.15. BOOK--Three authors

F   David Wallechinsky, Irving Wallace, and Amy Wallace, <u>The Book of Lists</u> (New York: William Morrow & Co., 1977), p. 15.

B   Wallechinsky, David; Wallace, Irving; and Wallace, Amy. <u>The Book of Lists</u>. New York: William Morrow & Co., 1977.

4.16. BOOK--More than three authors

F   Linda Micheli and others, <u>Managerial Communication</u> (Dallas: Scott, Foresman & Co., 1984), p. 211.

B   Micheli, Linda; Cepedes, Frank V.; Byker, Donald; and Raymond, Thomas J. C. <u>Managerial Communication</u>. Dallas: Scott, Foresman & Co., 1984.

4.17. BOOK--Editor as author

F   William T. Peck, ed., <u>Washington's Farewell Address</u> (New York: The Macmillan Company, 1909), pp. 17-26.

B   Peck, William T., ed. <u>Washington's Farewell Address</u>. New York: The Macmillan Company, 1909.

4.18. BOOK--Edited by a person other than the author

F   William Colburn and Sanford Weinberg, <u>An Orientation to Listening and Audience Analysis</u>. ed. by Ronald Applebaum and Roderick Hart (Chicago: Science Research Associates, 1980), p. 288.

B   Colburn, William, and Weinberg, Sanford. <u>An Orientation to Listening and Audience Analysis</u>. Edited by Ronald Applebaum and Roderick Hart. Chicago: Science Research Associates, 1980.

4.19. BOOK--Edition other than the first

F   Clarence Taber, <u>Taber's Cyclopedic Medical Dictionary</u>, 14th ed. (Philadelphia: F. A. Davis Co., 1981), p. 105.

B   Taber, Clarence Wilbur. <u>Taber's Cyclopedic Medical
     Dictionary</u>. 14th ed. Philadelphia: F. A. Davis
     Co., 1981.

4.20. REVIEW

F   N. Schedler, review of <u>Environmental Ethics</u>, by
     K. A. Shrader-Prechette, in <u>Defenders</u>, August 1982,
     p.33.

B   Schedler, N. Review of <u>Environmental Ethics</u>, by K. A.
     Shrader-Prechette. <u>Defenders</u>, August 1982, pp.
     33-34.

4.21. CITING WORK IN MORE THAN ONE VOLUME

F   Cyrus Hoy, <u>Introductions, Notes, and Commentar-
     ies to Texts in the Dramatic Works of Thomas Dekker</u>,
     vol. 1 (New York: Cambridge University Press, 1980),
     pp. 36-39.

B   Hoy, Cyrus. <u>Introductions, Notes, and Commentaries to
     Texts in the Dramatic Works of Thomas Dekker</u>.
     Vol. 1. New York: Cambridge University Press,
     1980.

4.22. ENCYCLOPEDIA ARTICLE--Author Listed

F   <u>McGraw-Hill Encyclopedia of Science and Tech-
     nology</u>, 1977 ed., vol. 12, S.v. "Sensory Learning," by
     Kao L. Chow.

B   <u>McGraw-Hill Encyclopedia of Science and Technology</u>,
     1977 ed. Vol. 12, S.v. "Sensory Learning," by Kao
     L. Chow.

4.23. ENCYCLOPEDIA ARTICLE--No author listed

F   <u>Encyclopedia Americana</u>, 1980 ed., s.v. "Navajo
     Mountain."

B   <u>Encyclopedia Americana</u>, 1980 ed. S.v. "Navajo Moun-
     tain."

4.24. GOVERNMENT DOCUMENT--Author listed

F   Mary C. Blehar, "Families and Public Policy,"
     <u>National Institute of Mental Health Monographs</u>. U.S.
     Department of Health, Education, and Welfare. (Wash-
     ington, DC: Government Printing Office, 1979), p. 26.

B   Blehar, Mary C. "Families and Public Policy." <u>National
     Institute on Mental Health Monographs</u>. Washing-
     ton, DC: U.S. Department of Health, Education,
     and Welfare, 1979.

4.25. GOVERNMENT DOCUMENT--No author listed

F   U.S. Department of Commerce, Bureau of the Cen-
     sus, <u>Statistical Abstract of the United States</u>. (Wash-
     ington, DC: Government Printing Office, 1979), pp. 321-
     23.

B   U. S. Department of Commerce, Bureau of the Census. <u>Sta-
    tistical Abstract of the United States.</u> Washing-
    ton, DC: Government Printing Office, 1979.

4.26. NEWSPAPER ARTICLE--Author listed
  F   Chris Hall, "Hunt's Lonely Climb to the Gover-
    nor's Mansion," <u>Montgomery Advertiser</u>, 10 December
    1986, Sec. C, p. 32.
  B   Hall, Chris. "Hunt's Lonely Climb to the Governor's
    Mansion," <u>Montgomery Advertiser</u>, 10 December
    1986, Sec. C, p. 32.

4.27. NEWSPAPER ARTICLE--No author listed
  F   "Perkins Resigns as Tide's Head Coach," <u>Mobile
    Press-Register</u>, 4 January 1987, Sec. D. p. 1.
  B   "Perkins Resigns as Tide's Head Coach," <u>Mobile Press-
    Register</u>, 4 January 1987.

4.28. EDITORIAL
  F   "Outrage Over Iranscam," Editorial. <u>New Orleans
    Times-Picayune</u>, 5 January 1987, p. 34.
  B   "Outrage Over Iranscam," Editorial, <u>New Orleans
    Times-Picayune</u>, 5 January 1987, p. 34.

4.29. PERIODICAL OR MAGAZINE ARTICLE--Author listed
  F   Christine Melnecki, "Jerome Frank: Persuader
    and Exemplar," <u>Journal of Counseling and Development</u>,
    65, January 1987, p. 228.
  B   Melnecki, Christine. "Jerome Frank: Persuader and Ex-
    emplar," <u>Journal of Counseling and Development</u>,
    65, January 1987, pp. 226-32.

4.30. PERIODICAL OR MAGAZINE ARTICLE--No author listed
  F   "Penn State Crowned National Champs," <u>The
    Sporting News</u>, 5 January 1987, p. 23.
  B   "Penn State Crowned National Champs." <u>The Sporting
    News,</u> 5 January 1987, p. 23.

    MISCELLANEOUS

4.31. BIBLE
  F   Psalm 105:15.
  B   The Bible, Revised Standard Version.

4.32. COLLECTED WORKS
  F   Morton N. Cohen, ed., <u>The Selected Letters of
    Lewis Carroll</u> (New York: Pantheon Books, 1982), p. 15.
  B   Cohen, Morton N., ed. <u>The Selected Letters of Lewis Car-
    roll</u>. New York: Pantheon Books, 1982.

4.33. DICTIONARY

  F   <u>Webster's New Collegiate Dictionary, 150th An-</u>
<u>niversary Edition</u> (Springfield, MA: The G. & C. Merriam
Co., 1981).

  B   <u>Webster's New Collegiate Dictionary, 150th Anniver-</u>
      <u>sary Edition</u>. (Springfield, MA: The G. & C. Mer-
      riam Co., 1981).

4.34. ERIC DOCUMENT

  F   Julie Thompson, <u>Sign Now Pay Later: Further Ex-</u>
<u>periments in Student Grading</u>, U.S. Educational Re-
sources Information Center, ERIC Document EJ 169 477,
1976.

  B   Thompson, Julie. <u>Sign Now Pay Later: Further Experi-</u>
      <u>ments in Student Grading</u>. U.S. Educational Re-
      sources Information Center, ERIC Document 169
      477, February 1976.

4.35. FILMSTRIP

  F   "Applying CPR," produced by the American Red
Cross, Instructional Media Center, 1986.

  B   "Applying CPR," produced by the American Red Cross In-
      structional Media Center, 1986.

4.36. ILLUSTRATIONS AND ART

  F   Taddeo Carlone, <u>Andrea Doria as Neptune</u>, 1599.
Marble. Villa Doria south garden (Allnari).

  B   Carlone, Taddeo. <u>Andrea Doria as Neptune</u>. 1599. Marble.
      Villa Doria south garden. (Allnari).

4.37. INSTRUCTIONAL MANUAL

  F   "Weight Control with Biofeedback," Instructional Manual, Montreal: Thought Technology Ltd.,
1984, p. 12.

  B   "Weight Control with Biofeedback." Instructional
      Manual. Montreal: Thought Technology Ltd.,
      1984.

4.38. INTERVIEW

  F   Interview with Arthur Outlaw, Mayor of Mobile at
City Hall, 2 January 1987.

  B   Outlaw, Arthur, Mayor of Mobile, Interview at City
      Hall, 2 January 1987.

4.39. LECTURE AND PRESENTATION

  F   Robert Ziller, "Social Psychology and Modern
Life," program presented at the Annual Meeting of the
Florida Psychological Association, Tallahassee, 15
July 1986.

B   Ziller, Robert. "Social Psychology and Modern Life."
     Program presented at the Annual Meeting of the
     Florida Psychological Association, Tallahas-
     see, 15 July 1986.

4.40. LETTER
F   Letter written by George A. Custer and on file in
     the National Archives, Washington, DC [n.d.].

B   Letter by George A. Custer on file in the National
     Archives, Washington, DC [n.d.].

4.41. LETTER to the EDITOR
F   Loren Spies, Letter, <u>Gainesville Sun</u> (12 January
     1987), p. 4.

B   Spies, Loren. Letter. <u>Gainesville Sun</u> (12 January
     1987).

4.42. PAMPHLET or BULLETIN in a SERIES
F   United Cerebral Palsy Association, <u>What Every-
     one Should Know About Cerebral Palsy</u> (New York: UCP
     Inc., 1977), p. 4.

B   United Cerebral Palsy Association. <u>What Everyone
     Should Know About Cerebral Palsy</u>. New York: UCP
     Inc., 1977.

4.43. POEM
F   John Greenleaf Whittier, "Snowbound," (Mount
     Vernon, NY: The Peter Paul Press, 1965), lines 1-2.

B   Whittier, John Greenleaf. "Snowbound." Mount Vernon,
     NY: The Peter Paul Press, 1965.

4.44. QUARTERLY
F   Arthur F. Burns, "U.S. Relations with West Ger-
     many," <u>The Atlantic Community Quarterly</u>, 20 (Summer
     1982): 153-57.

B   Burns, Arthur F. "U.S. Relations with West Germany,"
     <u>The Atlantic Community Quarterly</u>, 20 (Summer
     1982): 153-57.

4.45. RADIO and TELEVISION PROGRAM
F   "The Galen Hall Show," produced by the Florida
     Football Network, Inc., 11 November 1986.

B   "The Galen Hall Show," produced by the Florida Foot-
     ball Network, Inc., 11 November 1986.

4.46. TAPE RECORDING
F   Joseph Currier, <u>Less Stress</u>, produced by Listen &
     Learn USA!, 1986.

B   Currier, Joseph. <u>Less Stress</u>. Produced by Listen &
      Learn USA!, 1986.

4.47. TRANSLATION

F   Nicholas Yalouris, <u>Alexander the Great and His
      Heritage</u>, trans. David Hardy (Boston: New York Graphic
      Society, 1980), p. 22.

B   Yalouris, Nicholas. <u>Alexander the Great and His Heri-
      tage</u>. Translated by David Hardy. Boston: New York
      Graphic Society, 1980.

4.48. UNPUBLISHED DOCTORAL DISSERTATION

F   Anne F. Roberts, "Library Instruction for Li-
      brarians" (D.A. Dissertation, State University of New
      York at Albany, 1982), p. 15.

B   Roberts, Anne F. "Library Instruction for Librari-
      ans." D.A. Dissertation, State University of New
      York at Albany, 1982.

4.49. YEARBOOK ARTICLE

F   Marjorie Watson, "Mainstreaming the Educable
      Mentally Retarded," <u>Yearbook of Special Education</u>,
      1978-79 (Chicago: Marquis Who's Who, Inc., 1978), p.
      55.

B   Watson, Marjorie. "Mainstreaming the Educable Men-
      tally Retarded." <u>Yearbook of Special Education</u>,
      1978-79. Chicago: Marquis Who's Who, Inc., 1978.

These samples have been provided to show you the correct form for both footnote and bibliographic entry. Styles vary; however, be consistent in whatever style you use.

5

FOOTNOTING (continued), IN-TEXT DOCUMENTATION, and ENDNOTES

Footnotes add authority to what you say and are a vital part of your paper's documentation. Where they are used, accuracy, completeness, and consistency should prevail.

You will want to refer to Chapter 4 to see how footnote form differs from bibliographic form.

5.1. Footnotes have two purposes:
   a) To provide additional interesting information which is pertinent but not of primary importance.
   See Term Paper Page 4, footnote 4.
   b) To cite exact page references for quoted matter.
   See Term Paper Page 4, footnote 5.

5.2. Footnotes may be *simple* or *formal,* depending upon the wishes of your instructor, the style followed by your college, and the level of research undertaken in the paper.
   See Nos. 5.3–.4.

5.3. The simplified footnote style merely lists (a) the last name of the author, the title, and the exact page reference, or (b) the title, the reference, and page if the work is anonymous.
   Examples of simple style:
   a) [1] Current, *Mr. Lincoln,* p. 382.
   b) [2] *World Book Encyclopedia,* 1982 ed., s.v. Lincoln 12:285–86.
   See Term Paper Pages 3, 6, and 9.

5.4. The formal footnote style lists the full name (in signature order with family name last), title, volume number (if applicable), place of publication, publisher, date, and the exact page to which the reference is made.
   Example of formal footnote style:

¹ Richard N. Current, *Mr. Lincoln* (New York: Dodd, Mead and Co., 1957), p. 382.
See Term Paper Page 2; Nos. 4.13 F and B, 5.15.

5.5. The major purpose of a footnote is to direct the reader to the exact page reference. If your reader is satisfied with this and is content to get more detailed information in the bibliography at the end of the term paper, use the simplified style. If you think this style will be annoying, use the formal type of footnote. Check with your instructor first.
See No. 2.1.

5.6. A footnote cites the exact page reference, but the bibliography provides complete information about the reference. Every footnote must also have a bibliographic reference.
See Term Paper Page 3 and Bibliography.

5.7. Footnotes are punctuated like sentences. Phrases within them are separated by commas and they end with periods.
See Term Paper Page 3.

5.8. A primary footnote is formal and complete because it is making first reference to a work. Later references to the same work may use the simplified style.
See Term Paper Pages 3 and 8.

5.9. There are four acceptable methods for numbering footnotes:
    a) Continuous numbering throughout the paper (most common).
    b) Continuous numbering by page with each page starting with number 1 (common).
    c) Continuous numbering within each chapter (less common).
    d) In-text documentation with the footnotes appearing at the end of the paper (becoming common).
    See Nos. 5.25–.32.

The sample term paper at the end of this manual follows the style of (a) for footnoting.
Consult your instructor concerning which method to use.

5.10. Place the footnote on the same page as the material being cited.
See Term Paper Page 5.

5.11. If a footnote must be carried over to the next page, break it in the middle of the sentence and complete it at the bottom of the next page in the footnote position. Avoid breaking footnotes.
See Nos. 9.119–.120.

5.12. The number appearing at the *beginning* of the footnote is called a footnote number. Although it may be typed on the line, most style manuals suggest its being placed one-half space above the line.
See Term Paper Page 6.

5.13. The footnote number appearing at the *end* of the matter in the context appears one-half space above the line. It is called a superior number and is the same number as the one in the footnote to which it refers at the bottom of the page.
See Nos. 9.115, 9.125, and Term Paper Pages 12, 13.

5.14. The first line of the footnote is indented seven spaces from the left margin. All other lines for that footnote begin at the left margin.
See No. 4.12. F and Term Paper Page 4.

5.15. Footnotes are single-spaced and separated by one blank line.
See Term Paper Page 9.

5.16. There are two ways of separating the text from the footnotes:
   a) A solid line of underscores 1½ inches long extending from the left margin
   See Term Paper Page 6.
   b) A solid line of underscores extending from the left margin to the right margin
   The sample term paper uses the style described in (a).

5.17. Type the line of underscores either for (a) or (b) above, one or two spaces below the last line of context on the page, but be consistent.
See Nos. 9.76, 9.122, Term Paper Page 5.

5.18. Allow a minimum of one-half inch (3 lines) for every footnote. This allowance provides for the material as well as for the blank line above and below it for a one-line footnote.
See No. 9.117.

5.19. Shortcuts may be used to save time when more than one footnote refers to the same work.

The use of the Latin terms Ibid., loc. cit., op. cit., and idem help abbreviate the footnoting task. Such footnotes are used primarily by experienced research writers. Although there is a trend away from the use of Latin terms in footnoting, you will come upon such terms in your readings, and you should know what they mean. The use of "op. cit." and "loc. cit." is now obsolete. Avoid the overuse of Latin footnotes.
See Abbreviations Section Appendix D.

5.20. Ibid. refers to the immediately preceding footnote. It replaces the author's name and the title when both are the same as in the preceding footnote.
See No. 5.24 Footnotes 5, 6.
See Term Paper Pages 6, 9, 12.

5.21. Loc. cit. refers to the same reference. It is used when other footnotes intervene. Loc. cit. is preceded by the author's name. The page number is not given when using loc. cit.
See No. 5.24 Footnote 9.

5.22. Op. cit. refers to the work cited earlier. It eliminates the need for the title of the work. The author's name precedes op. cit., and the page reference follows it. Op. cit. is used when there are intervening footnotes. Op. cit. cites the same work but refers to a different page.
See No. 5.24 Footnote 8.

5.23. Idem sometimes replaces loc. cit. and op. cit. and means a name previously mentioned. It is used without an underscore or period. Use idem to refer to a previously mentioned name and when a footnote intervenes. However, the use of English rather than Latin is still preferred.
See No. 5.24 Footnote 10.

5.24. [4] John Cottrell, *Anatomy of an Assassination* (New York: Funk & Wagnalls, 1966), p. 92.
[5] Ibid.
(Refers to the immediately preceding title and to the same page.)
See Term Paper Pages 6, 9, 12.

⁶ Ibid., p. 115.

(Refers to the immediately preceding title but to a different page.)

See Term Paper Pages 9, 13.

⁷ Peter Farb, *Word Play* (New York: Alfred A. Knopf, 1974), p. 79.

⁸ Cottrell, *Anatomy*, p. 118. (Simplified footnote style using last name, short title, and page of work cited in footnote 4 but to a *different* page.) Or:

⁸ Cottrell, op. cit., p. 118. (Op. cit. may be used when there are intervening footnotes.) The use of op. cit. is discouraged for two reasons:

   a) The name of the work is not given, thus forcing the reader to check back for the title

   b) No space is saved

⁹ Farb, *Word Play*, p. 79. (Simplified footnote style instead of loc. cit.) Note that this footnote refers to the work cited in footnote 7 and to the *same* page. Or (but not preferred):

⁹ Farb, loc. cit. (Loc. cit. refers to the same work cited in footnote 7 and to the same page.) The use of loc. cit. is discouraged for the same reasons given in 8a and 8b above.

¹⁰ Cottrell, *Anatomy*, p. 121. (Simplified footnote style shown here refers to Cottrell's book cited in footnote 4 but to a *different* page.) This is the preferred style, but idem may be used when intervening footnotes occur. Or:

¹⁰ Idem, *Anatomy*, p. 121. (Refers to work cited in footnote 4 but to a different page.) Note how idem duplicates what op. cit. and loc. cit. do. However, the simplified footnote style shown immediately above is preferred.

IN-TEXT DOCUMENTATION

5.25. Increasing use is being made of in-text documentation because it offers several advantages:

   a) It eliminates the need to place footnotes at the bottom of the page.

   b) It is a short form for citing references.

   c) It allows the reader to see all the references on a single page.

   d) The references can be viewed side by side with each page of the term paper.

5.26. In-text documentation has several disadvantages:
  a) It is useful only when there are only two or three *different* references cited.
  b) Unless references are viewed side by side, the reader must turn to the back of the paper for a complete identification of the reference cited. This could be both annoying and distracting.

5.27. The value of in-text documentation lies in using an abbreviated form of footnoting. However, a full footnote (documentation) is required when the reference is first cited; when the same book is cited again, only the author's last name and the page number are given and this citation is made part of the contextual matter.
  See No. 5.29.

5.28. In-text documentation works best with only a few references. Any more than that and it becomes ungainly and borders on the risk of an incomplete or unclear documentation of the references cited.

5.29. Here is an example of in-text documentation as it might appear if used in the sample term paper:
  An interesting question as to why it took so long for Secretary Stanton to reply to the news of Booth's capture (Eisenschiml, p. 150) leads one to speculate about the Secretary of War and his reason for a delayed reaction to the news.
  Compare this in-text documentation paragraph example with the sample Term Paper, Page 15, Paragraph 2.

5.30. The example given in No. 5.29 cites only the author's name and the page reference because the book has already been cited in the paper with an accompanying full footnote. If in-text documentation were used, the Term Paper footnote, 24 on page 15 would not appear at the bottom of the page but at the end of the paper.

5.31. If you mention the name of the author in a sentence, list only the page number of the reference.
  Example: Eisenschiml speculates on Stanton's loyalty (150).

5.32. In-text documentation and endnotes are related, for if you use one, you must also use the other.

ENDNOTES

5.33. Styles vary as to how endnotes appear at the end of the paper. They are referred to by different names:
"Notes"
"Works Cited"

5.34. "Notes" rather than "Works Cited" is the more popular designation for the last page when in-text documentation is used.

5.35. The last page is headed "Notes" or "Works Cited"—*not* Bibliography.
See No. 9.129.

5.36. Endnotes consist of two kinds of information—a footnote citation (referent) and a content or explanatory statement.

5.37. A referent footnote identifies a book, periodical, etc.
See Nos. 4.12–.49.

5.38. A referent footnote must be included in the "Notes" section.

5.39. The sample term paper (Appendix B) cites eleven different references. This large number of different citations makes the use of endnotes impractical.
See No. 5.27–.28.

5.40. When using the endnote system, the first full reference to a citation appears at the bottom of the page; further references to the same work but not necessarily to the same page appear in the text and are enclosed in parentheses.
See 5.27–.30.

5.41. A content or explanatory note need not be included in the "Notes" section because while it may be of interest to the reader, it is not of prime importance to the paper. Practices vary on this point. Consult with your instructor.
See Nos. 2.1, 5.45.

5.42. A content or explanatory footnote elaborates, explains, questions, or calls attention to something.
See Term Paper, footnotes 4, 7, 9, and 15.

5.43. If the sample term paper footnotes 4, 7, and 15 were to be included in the "Notes" section, they would be complete sentences ending with periods.
See No. 5.45, footnote 3, 4.

5.44. Leave three blank lines after the heading "Notes" and then type your first endnote on the next line.
See No. 9.129.

5.45. Here is a sample of a portion of "Notes" as they would appear in place of a bibliography in the sample term paper. Use single or double spacing.

"Notes"

[2] Otto Eisenschiml, *Why Was Lincoln Murdered?* (New York: Grosset and Dunlap, 1937), pp. 12, 14.
[3] *World Book Encyclopedia,* 1982 ed., s.v. Lincoln 12:285–86.
[4] A single-shot, muzzle-loading, .41 caliber derringer pistol was used.
[5] U.S. Department of the Interior, *Lincoln Museum and the House Where Lincoln Died,* Booklet, reprint (Washington, DC: 1956), p. 14.

5.46. Notice the mix of referent (2, 3, 5) and content (4) footnotes. Also note that the page shows references in *footnote* form. There is *no* bibliography.

5.47. Before using the endnote system, consult with your instructor and obtain permission. Then, inquire about which type of endnote to include—referent, content, or both.
See Nos. 2.1, 2.22, 5.36–.42.

6

TAKING NOTES

Once you have developed an adequate bibliography, you are ready to take notes. Here is the heart of your research, so do not hurry it. Be sure to write plainly in order to avoid transcription errors later, and include a source reference on each card to simplify your footnoting task. *(See Chapter 3.)* Remember that the accuracy of the facts in your paper depends on the accuracy of your notes.

6.1. Prepare a preliminary or working bibliography for the purpose of recording information that might have value to your paper and is available in your library.
See Nos. 2.17, 4.1–4.8.

6.2. Develop an orderly, systematic, and scholarly routine for note-taking.
It is important that you include all pertinent information such as complete reference to the source. Before you leave the source, double-check the reference and content for accuracy. This will save time looking it up later.

6.3. You will take more notes than you need to complete your paper. It is better to have too much information, which can be pruned for basic essentials, than to have so little that you must search for more at the last minute.

6.4. Be critical of what you read, and write sparingly, keeping your notes to a minimum.

6.5. Using 5 × 8 white lined cards for note-taking makes it easy to sort, eliminate, and arrange data into logical sequence. It is not always possible to tell what is relevant as you take notes.
Even though some of your notes may seem to have little value, do not dispose of them. Put them in a separate pack and label HOLD just in case you need them later.

6.6. Use a larger-size card for note-taking to avoid mix-up with the smaller bibliographic cards.

6.7. Carry spare cards with you at all times, as evidence sometimes presents itself in strange places.

6.8. Avoid unusual abbreviations as a form of shorthand in note-taking, for you run the risk of failing to transcribe accurately, particularly when a quotation is involved.

6.9. Write on one side of the card. If you must continue onto a second card, write "continued" at the top and number each card such as 1A, 1B.
    See No. 6.17.

6.10. Place only one idea on each card.
    See No. 6.11.

6.11. Notes may be of the following types: quotation, paraphrase, personal comment.
    See examples following No. 6.16.

6.12. At the top center of each card, on the red line, write the type of note you are making.
    See Nos. 6.11–.18.

6.13. Each card should have a descriptive label consisting of a main heading and subheading.
    See Nos. 6.11–.18.

6.14. Each card contains three essential items of information:
    Reference to the source
    Descriptive label
    Body
    See Nos. 6.11–.18.

6.15. Read the reference thoroughly before writing your note and then digest what you have read into one key idea.

6.16. Notes which summarize, comment upon the text, and/or evaluate what you have read are superior to quotation notes because more of YOU is put into the paper and that is what your instructor desires.

Quotation .IIA

Lincoln's fears of acts against his life
" philosophy on his own safety
"No use in worrying. What is to be
must be. If anyone is really
determined to kill me, I shall be
killed!"

→ Outline
Placement
Code
(See 6.3.)

Paraphrase IIB

Security Measures
Parker, Metropolitan policeman
            appointed guard
Mrs. Lincoln dismissed the regular
guard. She then requested that
Parker be assigned the special task
of guarding the President. It is
assumed that Mrs. Lincoln did
not know about Parker's reputation for drunkenness while on
duty, unbecoming conduct, and
being AWOL from his past.
            Eisenschiml p 12, 14

→ Descriptive
Label

→ Short
Reference

Personal Comment IIC

Invitation for Ford theatre
            Performance
Difficult in securing acceptance

→ Body

[It seems incredible the Pres. of
the U.S. found it difficult to
find someone willing to accept
a Presidential invitation to
sit in the Presidential Box
during the performance]

[Is it of interest to know more
about Clara Harris who
accepted the invitation?]
            Eisenschiml p12

6.17. Recording essential information when you are reading a reference for the purpose of taking notes will save you time later.
Then you will not have to go back in the final stages of your

work when you are writing or typing the paper to obtain facts which are so easily obtainable during note-taking.

Identify sources of information in the short reference form (see paraphrase card shown above) by including the author's last name unless your bibliography lists more than one book by the same name, or more than one person with the same last name. The example shown here is Eisenschiml, pp. 12, 14.

6.18. Identify facts and opinions in your notes. If the author expresses a personal opinion, record it as such in your notes and preface his opinion with the phrase, "according to the author," or some similar phrase.

6.19. Facts of common knowledge need not be documented. Such statements as "John Wilkes Booth killed the President" and "Abraham Lincoln was President during the American Civil War" are common knowledge and need not be documented or carry a footnote reference.

6.20. Statements (a) which have questionable validity and/or (b) are controversial in nature, and/or (c) which contain little-known facts must be documented.

   a) Statements open to question should be documented. For example, "Large doses of Vitamin C will prevent colds" is not a proven fact; it would be necessary and important to know who said it, since the medical profession is divided on the subject.

   b) A controversial statement, such as "The seat belt law is an invasion of a person's constitutional right to privacy" needs to be documented.

   c) A little-known fact, such as "Many of the Indians who massacred General Custer and his 7th Cavalry were armed with repeater rifles while the soldiers had only single-shot rifles to defend themselves" should be documented.

6.21. Laws and formulas should appear as quotations.

6.22. Copy quotations exactly including punctuation, spelling, capitalization, paragraphing, and errors.

6.23. If you note an error in your reference and you wish to call this error to the attention of your reader, copy the quotation exactly

as it appears in the original, follow the error with the word *sic* placed in brackets, and then make the correction.
See No. 9.55.

6.24. Use quotations only when you wish to retain the exact wording of the author because his statement is not clear, is of great significance, or is of a challenging nature.
See Term Paper Page 6.

6.25. Ellipses are used to indicate the omission of a few words from a quotation when such omissions are irrelevant to your subject.
See Term Paper Page 9.
  a. Use three spaced dots when the omission is at the beginning or in the middle of a sentence.
  b. Use three spaced dots plus a period (four spaced dots) when the omission occurs at the end of a sentence.
  See Term Paper Page 9, Nos. 9.77–.82.

6.26. When ellipses end a quotation, place the ellipses inside the quotation mark.

6.27. Indicate the omission of an entire paragraph or more by a full line of double-spaced periods (ellipses).
See Term Paper Pages 9, 12, No. 9.81.

6.28. When you wish to insert your own words within a quotation, place brackets [ ] around your words.
See Term Paper Pages 3, 7, No. 9.62.

6.29. When you wish to clarify but not within a quotation, enclose the word in parentheses.
See Term Paper Page 3, No. 9.66.

6.30. If you need to write a précis (pronounced pray-*see)* you are reporting in your own words on a longer piece of something you have read. Your précis gets to the core on this longer piece; you report from the author's viewpoint and not from your own. The précis is a brief summary of the main points or facts. See how it differs from a thesis statement.
See Nos. 2.18–.19.

6.31. Keep your completed notes on file until your term paper has been returned by your instructor.

7

MAKING THE OUTLINE

After you have prepared your note cards, you are ready to make your first outline. It may be necessary to revise this outline several times. Work it out with great care, for you are only one step away from writing the first draft of your paper.

7.1. An outline enumerates important ideas to be developed in the paper. Review your thesis statement.
See Nos. 2.18–.19.

7.2. An outline keeps you from wandering by forcing you to clarify your thinking about your subject.
As your outline begins to develop, gaps in your research (note-card information) will be apparent and you will then see where additional research is needed.

7.3. There is a relationship between the outline and the note cards. The usual procedure is to base the outline on the note cards. It is better to prepare the outline after the notes have been completed, even though it *is* possible to prepare the outline before taking your notes. Refer to the three note cards in No. 6.16. The outline placement code appearing in the upper right-hand corner of each card was placed there to signify the order in which the note cards were arranged. The quotation card was assigned the code IIA, the paraphrase card was given the outline code IIB, and the personal comment card was assigned 11C.
See No. 6.17 and the topic and sentence outline in No. 7.13.

7.4. If you prepare your outline from your notes, you may want to spread your note cards on the floor and put them back together again in logical order.

7.5. An outline should provide a guide for writing a term paper. It may list items in their order of time occurrence.
If the term paper is on Lincoln's assassination, your *first* outline might appear as follows:

LINCOLN'S ASSASSINATION
I. Before the assassination
II. The assassination
III. After the assassination

7.6. An outline may also develop by expanding the main thought without regard to chronological arrangement.

LINCOLN'S ASSASSINATION—AN UNSOLVED MYSTERY
I. The act itself
II. Grant's strange behavior
III. Mrs. Lincoln's unfortunate choice of bodyguard
IV. The President's premonition
V. Booth's strange revelations

7.7. Your outline can change to suit your purpose. You are not shackled to the first one you prepare. Constant revision of your outline will develop it to full maturity.

Note how the outlines on Lincoln's assassination in Nos. 7.5–.6, 7.11, and the topic and sentence outline in 7.13 change as they mature.

7.8. The outline must indicate a reason for your paper. It must show relationships between facts, and it must come to a logical conclusion.

Avoid words like Introduction, Body, and Summary in your outline. They are vague and do not contribute to the development of your paper. Specific headings are needed.

7.9. Avoid too many main headings, but have at least three.

The following outline form illustrates too fine a breakdown:

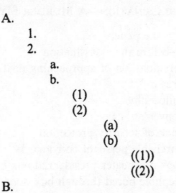

I.
  A.
    1.
    2.
      a.
      b.
        (1)
        (2)
          (a)
          (b)
            ((1))
            ((2))
  B.

7.10. If you list a I, you must also have a II. This is true for all subdivisions.

7.11. All main headings such as I, II, and III should be of the same value.

Unequal headings   *Equal headings*

LINCOLN'S ASSASSINATION
  I. Events leading to the murder
 II. The murder
III. Confusing news reports
 IV. Sergeant Cobb
  V. Patrolman Parker

LINCOLN'S ASSASSINATION
  I. Events leading to the murder
 II. The murder
III. Booth's escape
 IV. Booth's accomplices

7.12. Have all periods in main heading numbers line up. This also applies to all subdivisions.

7.13. Although a topic outline is easier to prepare, a sentence outline is preferred because it makes the writer really think about his or her subject and will result in an easier task and a superior paper.

    Notice in the following partial outlines how the sentence outline brings the student closer to the point of writing his or her paper.

TOPIC OUTLINE

LINCOLN'S ASSASSINATION—A MURDER MYSTERY

  I. Purpose of the paper
 II. Lincoln—before the assassination
   A. His premonition of approaching death
     1. Dreams
     2. Philosophy
     3. Conversations
   B. His lack of security protection
     1. Unreliable personal bodyguard
     2. Lock on theater presidential box broken
     3. Peephole bored through box door undetected

C. His difficulty in obtaining guests for the performance
  1. Grant to be honored with Lincoln at theater
  2. Grant accepts President's invitation
  3. Grant declines invitation
  4. Lincoln finds himself without guests
III. The assassination
  A. A look at the assassin
  B. Motives for murder
  C. The shooting
  D. Stanton's famous last words
IV. After the assassination
  A. Booth's escape into Maryland
    1. Passed through guard post
    2. Received medical aid from physician
    3. Hidden by southern sympathizers
  B. Stanton's lack of co-operation
    1. Refused to give Booth's name to press
    2. Disinterested in capture of John Surrat
  C. The accomplices
  D. The trial

The final outline appears in sentence form. Every heading and subdivision is a complete statement.

SENTENCE OUTLINE*

LINCOLN'S ASSASSINATION—A MURDER MYSTERY

I. The purpose of this paper is to identify unexplained events in connection with the death of Abraham Lincoln.
  A. Records of the assassination reveal gaps and inconsistencies of the events leading up to and following the murder.
  B. John Wilkes Booth killed Lincoln, but why he did it and the full details of his diabolical plan leave many questions unanswered.
II. Lincoln had been marked for death by several people dur-

* See Term Paper Pages 1, 2, 3 and note how this sentence outline develops into paragraphs to become a term paper.

ing his term in office, but efforts to protect his life went unnoticed.

A. Before his death, Lincoln had suspected that he would be killed at the hands of an assassin.

    1. He was extremely melancholy on the day of the shooting, having been troubled by bad dreams.

    2. His philosophy on his own safety reflected a fatalistic attitude.

    3. He said "good-bye" rather than "good night" as he left the White House for the theater.

B. The President was not provided with adequate security measures.

    1. The regular guard was dismissed and a discredited police officer was assigned to guard his life.

        a. Patrolman Parker had been officially reprimanded for drunkenness on several occasions.

        b. Parker had been found guilty of conduct unbecoming an officer on several occasions.

        c. Parker had been known to leave his post without proper leave on several occasions.

    2. The lock on the door leading to the presidential box was broken.

    3. A peephole that had been bored in the door leading to the presidential box went unnoticed.

7.14. If asked, submit your outline to your instructor for his or her approval. You may save yourself time and heartache.

8

WRITING THE PAPER

Very few people are naturally gifted writers. For most of us, writing is a difficult task. To do a creditable job it will be necessary for you to rework paragraphs and labor over some of your sentences as you try to find the word that expresses the precise thought you have in mind. Above all, do not get discouraged now. Other students are going through the same experience and those who persevere and rise above their discouragements will finally achieve their goal, a term paper of which they can be proud. **Before writing your paper, review the Term Paper Checklist in Appendix C.**

8.1. Do not delay writing until the last possible moment. You cannot do a good job if you rush it. Allow yourself ample time.

8.2. Keep within the number of words set for your paper by your instructor.

A minimum of 2,000 words is usually required.
See No. 2.1.

8.3. Choose a tentative title that is interesting, clear, and brief. Your completed (final) paper may indicate a need to reword the title. Your final title may be your *last* task in completing the typing of your paper.

8.4. Your instructor will probably be influenced by your opening and closing paragraphs, so make them especially good.
See No. 8.52.

8.5. Not even the most experienced writer can hope that the first draft will be the best. Prepare yourself to do several typed drafts before your paper is in its final form.

8.6. During your first draft, review your thesis statement. Start writing and do not be concerned with grammar or sentence construction. You can correct this later. The important thing is to *get started.*
See Nos. 2.18, 8.52.

8.7. Avoid merely copying your notes. This makes the reading dull, choppy, and lacks the most essential element, YOU.

8.8. Avoid colloquialisms and slang expressions.

8.9. If you have a choice between using a simple word or a technical one, choose the simpler word your reader will understand.
His remuneration for the week was in excess of $200.
His pay for the week was more than $200.

8.10. Try to avoid making any personal references to yourself such as *I, me, mine,* or *the writer.* Keep personal pronouns out of the paper if possible.

8.11. Have a dictionary and a thesaurus handy and consult them.

8.12. Write the first draft with your notes and outline before you. Use the outline as your writing guide and your notes to recall the facts. If you make changes in your paper, adjust your outline accordingly as they must be reconciled.
See No. 8.52.

8.13. Use wide margins and triple space your first draft to allow room for corrections.

8.14. Use separate sheets of paper for each paragraph in your draft. This will allow you to add to your paragraphs during your revision and to insert footnotes without fear of crowding your work.

8.15. Write or type on one side of 8½- by 11-inch paper which is of quality good enough to take erasing and editing.

8.16. Prepare a carbon copy or photocopy in case your instructor wishes to see your draft. Term papers *have* been lost.

8.17. If asked, submit a clean copy of your revised draft to your instructor. Type it if possible.

8.18. Allow one-half inch (three lines) for each footnote.
See Nos. 9.116–.118.

8.19. Documenting and footnoting are closely related. To document means to place a number one-half space above the line *after* the passage you wish to be identified as a footnote. This number is called a superior or superscript number. The same number is

used to identify the footnote. It also apears one-half space above the line and immediately *preceding* the footnote.
See Nos. 5.3–.5, 5.12–.13 and Term Paper Page 8.

8.20. Document and footnote as you write your draft. You might forget one or the other if you hold off doing this until your final copy is being prepared. *(See Chapters* 4 and 5 for the form and content of footnotes.)

8.21. When using a quotation, work it into the text smoothly with a transitional sentence.
See Term Paper Page 10.

8.22. Quoted matter should not take up more than one fifth of your paper. The remainder of your text comes from your own ideas.

8.23. Avoid using quoted matter unless it is absolutely essential that the words of another be included.

8.24. Long quotations do not have quotation marks, are single spaced and indented five spaces from the left and right margins of the context.
See Nos. 9.130–.133, and Term Paper Page 8.

8.25. Rather than copy a quotation, staple or clip the quotation note card and your typed footnote to your draft. This saves time when you type your final draft and ensures against error and also shows you how much space to leave for footnotes in the final copy.
See Nos. 9.116–.118.

8.26. Acknowledge all paraphrases by using a superior number (raised one-half space) after the material and then listing it in the footnotes. Don't pass someone else's ideas off as your own.
See Term Paper Page 6, No. 9.115.

8.27. Determine whether the paragraphs of your first draft are in logical order. If not, change them.

8.28. Every paragraph should have a key, or topic sentence—usually at its beginning.
See Term Paper Pages 6, 7.

8.29. Have medium and short paragraphs for interest.

8.30. If you include a summary paragraph, it should be short and concise and should answer the question in your opening paragraph, if that is the way your paper begins.
See Term Paper Page 16.

8.31. After writing the paper, lay it aside for at least a day. Then when your outlook is fresh, pick it up and criticize it *severely*. If the instructor has given you a guide sheet of "Do's and Dont's", review it carefully as you edit your draft. It is far better for you to do this than to have constructive criticisms come from your instructor for that is the instructor's role in helping you improve your writing and research skills.
See No. 8.34 and Term Paper Checklist, Appendix C.

8.32. Internally examine the paper for unity, tense, coherence, and structure. Ask yourself:
Does the central theme hold together well?
Does the paper express itself clearly?
Is the paper well put together grammatically?
Other questions which will help you evaluate your paper can be found in the term paper checklist following the sample term paper. *See Appendix C.*

8.33. It may be necessary for you to clip and paste your first draft in different order for a more logical arrangement.
From your pasted draft, prepare your final copy.

8.34. Review and edit the final draft before typing the copy which you will submit to your instructor. This means that you may need to correct grammar, switch paragraphs, change words, delete irrelevant material, sharpen sentences to avoid rambling, improve your writing style, add tables and graphics, and rework your title.
See No. 8.43–.47 A, B, C, D.

8.35. Check all footnotes and bibliographic entries for consistency of form and to see that all essential information is included.
See Nos. 4.12–.49 and Chapter 5.

8.36. Through constant pruning of irrelevant material, you may find your final copy shorter than your draft copy.

8.37. If the final copy does not sound like you, the difference will be noted by your instructor. Now, while you can still make changes, be yourself but use acceptable grammar.

8.38. The finished paper may include a title page (optional), text, and bibliography.
See Nos. 9.38–.39 and Term Paper Title Page.

8.39. If a table of contents is needed, your outline, slightly revised, will serve the purpose. A table of contents is usually not necessary; its main use is in very long papers such as theses and dissertations. If a table of contents *is* needed, you will also need a title page.

8.40. Remove from your note cards material you do not use in the paper and keep these extra notes securely bound in a separate pack. You may want to refer to them later.

8.41. Save your note cards, because your instructor may wish to examine them.

8.42. If you mount illustrations in your paper, use rubber cement to prevent wrinkling.

8.43. If tables, charts, or graphics are to be included in your paper, remember that their only purpose is to communicate ideas, so keep them simple.

8.44. Each table, chart, or graph is most effective when it presents only one idea.

8.45. Each table, chart, and graph should be so simple that its meaning is immediately clear to the reader.
See No. 8.44.

8.46. Tables, charts, and graphs need some type of linkage, and this can be accomplished by the use of a transitional sentence that works the illustration gracefully into its proper place in the paper.

8.47. Table numbers and titles appear above the table. Names and titles of other graphics appear below the illustration.
See No. 8.44.

A

Table 1
*Population of the U.S.
in Five Different Time Periods*

YEAR	POPULATION*	
1800	5.3	
1850	23.1	
1900	76.2	
1950	151.3	
2000	269.	(Est.)

* Expressed in millions

SOURCE: *The World Almanac and Book of Facts,* 1987,
p. 219.

B

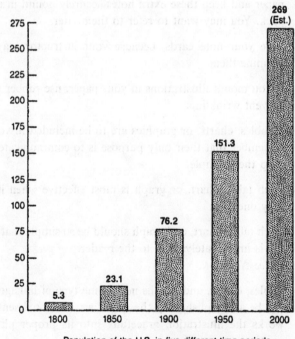

Population of the U.S. in five different time periods
(Expressed in millions)

SOURCE: *The World Almanac and Book of Facts,* 1987, p. 219.

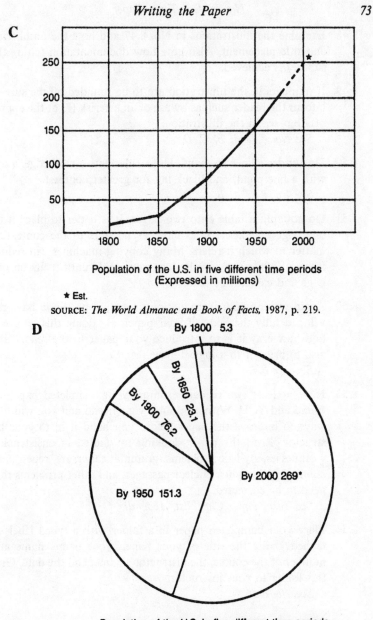

C

Population of the U.S. in five different time periods
(Expressed in millions)

★ Est.

SOURCE: *The World Almanac and Book of Facts,* 1987, p. 219.

D

By 1800 5.3

By 1850 23.1

By 1900 76.2

By 1950 151.3

By 2000 269*

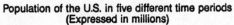

Population of the U.S. in five different time periods
(Expressed in millions)

* Est.

SOURCE: *The World Almanac and Book of Facts,* 1987, p. 219.

8.48. Examine the illustrations in No. 8.47 and note the numbering and title placement. Also note how documentation (citing the source) is achieved.

8.49. If numbers in the illustration are to be rounded off, be sure to inform the reader such as by use of an asterisk (*) at the appropriate place in the illustration.
See No. 8.47 A, B, C, D.

8.50. Do not draw lines freehand. Use a ruler with a steel edge, a pen with a fine point, and black ink for greater contrast.
See No. 8.47 A, B, C, D.

8.51. Do not split a table onto two pages. It is better to place it on one page and insert it as close as possible to the contextual matter to which it refers. Many copying machines can reduce material while copying. Reduce your table until it fits on one page and can still be read.

8.52. Avoid writing your introduction or ending until you have developed fully the body of your paper. By doing this, you will find how easy it is to introduce your paper to the reader and also to bring it to a logical close.
See No. 8.4.

8.53. Have at least two readers examine your completed paper—a friend and YOU. Without doubt, your friend and you will find ways to improve the paper before you hand it in to your instructor. Read the paper, looking for faults, inconsistencies, weaknesses, stylistic problems, grammatical errors, repetitions, conflicting thoughts, unclear passages, and other problems that need to be corrected.
See Term Paper Checklist, Appendix C.

8.54. Place your completed paper in a folder with a typed label attached giving the title of your paper, your name, name and number of the course, the instructor's name, and the date. Give this folder to your instructor.
See No. 8.16.

9

TYPING THE PAPER

The end is in sight but don't spoil all you have done by passing in your paper prematurely. Be proud but be careful! DON'T submit a handwritten copy, as it will be difficult to read. But if you must, is your handwriting legible? Even more important, modern communication skills are upgraded to typed and word-processed documents. Do yourself a special favor and hand in a clean, carefully typed, error-free, attractive term paper correct in mechanics and submitted on time. Even if you have your paper done on a word processor it is important for you to read this chapter.

This chapter is divided into three sections: What to Do Before Typing Your Paper (9.1–.45), Typing Your Paper (9.46-.141), and After Typing Your Paper (9.142–.147).

WHAT TO DO BEFORE TYPING

9.1. A primary consideration is the kind of typewriter you will use. Modern electric and electronic typewriters have many special keys and features not available on the older standard and portable-size manual typewriters. Special keys and features found on some of the newer typewriters include: boldface type, italics, square brackets, accent marks, and special character keys. Other features include: easy change from elite- to pica-size type, interchangeable type style, automatic recall of paragraphs and pages, lift-off memory correction, built-in character display before letters are typed, built-in word dictionary, end-of-page warning signal, automatic page numbering, fast forward, underlining, and vertical and backward spacing.

9.2. Unless your instructor specifies otherwise, follow the general style suggestions offered in this manual.

9.3. Read this chapter in its entirety before typing your paper.

9.4. Lend this manual to your typist to use as a guide in typing your paper, paying particular attention to this chapter and also to the sample term paper, Appendix B.

9.5. Use a cleaning agent (fluid, special putty, blotters) to clean your typewriter keys. No one likes to read a paper where individual letters such as a, o, d, b, c, p, or e are completely blocked.

9.6. If you will submit your paper in a folder, purchase the folder before typing so as to determine what margins you will need. *See No. 9.33.*

Paper Selection

9.7. Type on white, 8½ by 11-inch bond with a rag content of 50 percent.

9.8. Avoid the use of thesis paper. The use of such paper could be interpreted as "putting on airs." Use plain bond.

9.9. Avoid using a coated or erasable paper, as it tends to smudge ink and type.

Type Size and Style

9.10. It makes little difference whether you use elite- or pica-size type. Avoid using micro or script, as they are more difficult to read.

9.11. To identify type size, look at the scale of numbers below the cylinder or above the keyboard. Elite scales usually run from zero to 130 or more. Pica scales range from zero to 85 or more.

Paper Size and Lines

9.12. Use paper 8½ by 11 inches in size. Set your typewriter line spacer so that you will have six vertical lines to the vertical inch. Therefore, paper 11 inches long has the capability of having 66 typed lines. However, you will not use all these lines because you will have top and bottom margins. *See Nos. 9.24b, 9.33.*

Handwritten Copy

9.13. If you handwrite your paper, use white paper with ruled lines one-half inch apart. Avoid submitting a handwritten copy.

9.14. Black ink is the only acceptable color for handwritten papers.

9.15. If someone is going to type from your handwritten copy, go over the draft with that person to clarify spellings and writing that may not be legible. This is especially important for quoted matter and footnotes.

Typed Copy

9.16. If you type your paper, use a new ribbon (black) for the best possible contrast.

9.17. Prepare a carbon or a machine copy. Papers *do* get lost!

9.18. Type on one side of the paper.

9.19. Set your line spacer for double spacing. Double spacing means you have one blank line between every typed line.

Making Corrections

9.20. Rules concerning how many and what kinds of errors can be tolerated on a single page vary considerably. Some instructors are more lenient than others. Some instructors allow errors to be corrected neatly with pen and ink; other instructors do not. When errors occur, they must be corrected. You have several options:
   a. Pen-and-ink corrections made above the line with the use of the caret ∧.
      See No. 9.57.
   b. Erase error and retype. Avoid.
      See No. 9.22.
   c. Use correcting paper to cover error and retype.
      See No. 2.1, 2.22 (question 9).
   d. Retype page.

9.21. Strikeovers are never permitted. Misspelled words, letters omitted within words, omitted words, and the same word typed twice by error must be corrected. If you cannot make a neat and attractive correction, retype the page.
      See No. 9.23.

9.22. The use of specially treated correcting paper is preferred to erasing. Erasures, improperly made, are unsightly and may result in a hole in the paper. An inexpensive package of correcting slips is available in any stationery store.

9.23. Learn how to delete and add a letter to a word by removing the word with a correcting slip, repositioning the line, and retyping.

Guide and Border Sheet

9.24. This sheet, which you will design, will help you keep within the margins. It will also help you estimate how many lines must be saved for footnotes. The sheet is placed directly behind the typing paper. When fully designed, it measures 9 by 11 inches which is one-half inch wider than typing paper but of the same length. Here is how you make a *Guide and Border Sheet:*

   a. Examine the sample shown on page 79.

   b. Select a regular 8½ by 11-inch sheet of paper. Use a broad marking pen (black) and draw the margins: left margin 1½ inches. Top, bottom and right margins 1 inch.
See No. 9.33.

   c. Using another sheet of paper, insert it into the typewriter. About 1 inch from the right edge and beginning at the very top line, type the figure 66. One line directly below that, type 65. Continue this subtracting and typing process to the very bottom line where you will type the figure 1.

   d. Cut this strip of numbers from the paper leaving one-half inch extra to the left of the numbers for gluing. Using rubber cement, paste this overlap to the right side of your typing paper on which you have drawn the margins in the shape of a rectangle. You now have a *Guide and Border Sheet* that is 9 inches wide and 11 inches long. When placed directly behind your typing paper, the numbers you have typed will extend beyond your 8½ by 11-inch typing sheet and thus be visible to you. You can see by a glance at any time how many line spaces are left on the paper.
See No. 9.25.

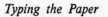

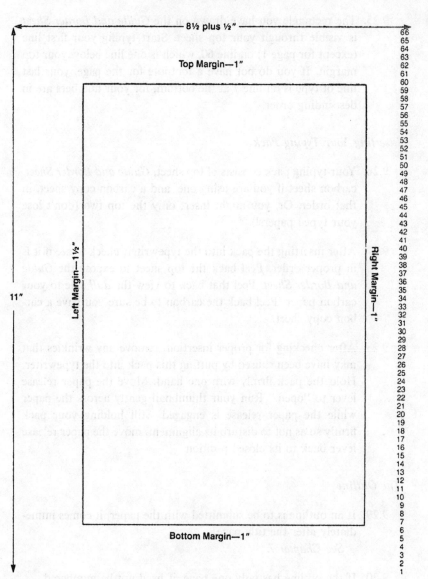

8½ plus ½"

Top Margin—1"

Left Margin—1½"

Right Margin—1"

11"

Bottom Margin—1"

9.25. The rectangle you have drawn on the *Guide and Border Sheet* is visible through your top sheet. Start typing your first line (except for page 1) on line 60, which is one line below your top margin. If you do not have a footnote for the page, your last line of type is on line 7 at the bottom, for your numbers are in descending order.

Inserting Your Typing Pack

9.26. Your typing pack consists of top sheet, *Guide and Border Sheet,* carbon sheet if you are using one, and a carbon copy sheet, in that order. Or, you might insert only the top two (don't lose your typed papers!).

9.27. After inserting the pack into the typewriter, check to see if it is in proper order. Peel back the top sheet to expose the *Guide and Border Sheet.* Peel that back to view the *dull* side to your carbon paper. Peel back the carbon to be sure you have a carbon copy sheet.

9.28. After checking for proper insertion, remove any wrinkles that may have been caused by putting this pack into the typewriter. Hold the pack firmly with one hand. Move the paper release lever to "open." Run your thumbnail gently across the paper while the paper release is engaged. Still holding your pack firmly so as not to disturb its alignment, move the paper release lever back to its closed position.

The Outline

9.29. If an outline is to be submitted with the paper, it comes immediately after the title page.
See Chapter 7.

9.30. If the outline has only one page, it need not be numbered.

9.31. If the outline contains more than one page, the first page is numbered at the bottom center one inch above the margin with i. Page 2 of the outline will be numbered ii; and so forth.

Margins

9.32. If the paper will not be placed in a folder or cover, set your margins as indicated in No. 9.24b.

9.33. If your paper will be inserted into a three-hole cover, have a left margin of two inches.

9.34. It is all right to be one line over or under your bottom margin but any more of a variance will result in a crowded or a "short" page. Avoid this problem by using your *Guide and Border Sheet.*
    See No. 9.25.

Pagination

9.35. The first page of your term paper is usually not numbered although it does count as page one. All succeeding pages are numbered in the upper right corner one-half inch from the top edge (three lines) and one inch from the right edge. If numbered properly, the page numbers will dance before your eyes if you rapidly fan the pages.
    See Term Paper Pages 1 and 2.

9.36. If page one is numbered (not a common practice) the number appears at the bottom center one inch above the margin (bottom line 7).

9.37. Page numbers do not have anything preceding or following; simply type the number without any embellishment.
    See Term Paper Page 2.

Title Page

9.38. The title page contains the title of the paper, the word "by" (optional), your name, the name and/or course number, your instructor's name, and the date you submit the paper, in that order. Type title on line 23.
    See Term Paper Title Page.

9.39. Some term papers do not have a title page. If this is acceptable to your instructor, here is what you do: An alternative to having a title page is to use the upper right corner of the first page of your paper to give the following information (use single or double spacing):

> Your name
> Name of course
> Number of course
> Course section number
> Name of instructor
> Date

Triple-space after the date and center your title. Capitalize only the major words; place articles and prepositions in small letters (lower case). Do not underline. Triple-space again, reset your margins for double-spacing, and begin typing your paper.
See Nos. 2.1, 2.22.

9.40. Avoid decorative designs on the title page.
See Term Paper Title Page.

9.41. The title is typed in capital letters on the title page.
See Term Paper Title Page.

Page One

9.42. If you have a title page, your title will also appear on page 1. Leave a top margin of three inches (18 lines) and type the title centered and capitalized. This title is on line 48 (See right side of your *Border and Guide Sheet).*
See No. 9.44 and Term Paper Page 1.

9.43. If you handwrite your paper, the title appears in the same position as described in No. 9.42. Capitalize only the first letter and do not underline.

9.44. After typing the title on page 1, space down three or four lines to begin typing the first line of your paper. Watch your *Guide and Border Sheet* numbers so that you will begin typing on approximately line 44. Use double spacing.
See No. 9.42 and Term Paper Page 1.

Body of the Paper

9.45. The body of the paper is double-spaced, but quotations longer than three lines and the bibliography are single-spaced.
See Nos. 9.130–.131, Term Paper Page 3 and Bibliography.

TYPING THE PAPER

Some instructors want term papers double-spaced throughout including footnotes and bibliography. Ask your instructor about this before typing your paper.
See Nos. 2.1, 2.22.

The Last Page

9.46. Do not type "The End" at the end of the paper.
See Term Paper Page 17.

9.47. If the last page contains a footnote, *see No. 9.128.*

Dividing Words

9.48. Avoid dividing words, if possible, especially on two succeeding lines. Consult a dictionary for correct word division.

9.49. Avoid dividing a word on the last line of a page, as this would mean a "carryover" to the next page.

Dividing Sentences

9.50. Avoid, if possible, carrying sentences to the next page if it means only a one- or two-word carryover.

Dividing Paragraphs

9.51. Plan your typing so that you do not have a paragraph that begins on the bottom line. It is better to place the entire paragraph on the next page.

Paragraphs

9.52. If your paper has paragraph headings, underline the words and spaces and type the paragraph flush with the left margin.
See Term Paper Page 2.

9.53. Indent the first line of the paragraph 5 spaces and begin typing.
See Term Paper Page 2.

9.54. Double-space between paragraphs. This means you have one blank line between paragraphs.
See Term Paper Page 15.

Sic

9.55. The Latin word <u>sic</u> is enclosed in square brackets and is used to indicate that something has been copied exactly as in the original including untruths, word omissions, and errors in grammar and spelling. Underline sic.
See No. 6.23 and Abbreviations, Appendix D.

Ibid.

9.56. Type the word with a capital I, end with a period, and do not underline.
See Term Paper Page 12.

Caret ∧

9.57. Use a caret ∧ at the appropriate place within a word or between words to indicate that a missing letter or word is being added.
See No. 9.20a.

Typing the Figure 1

9.58. Older typewriter keyboards usually do not have the figure 1 key; use a lowercase letter 1 (el) that is to the immediate right of the k key. Do not use the capital I as it looks like the Roman numeral I.
See Term Paper Title Page.

Poetry

9.59. If you quote poetry, separate it from the text by indenting and single spacing it. Type it using the same line length as in the original and place it one double space below your contextual matter. Do not enclose in quotation marks.
See No. 9.82.

Punctuation

The following section lists the most common usages of punctuation marks. **Consult a dictionary for more complete information.**

Square Brackets [ ]

9.60. Older typewriters usually do not have a square bracket key. Brackets can be drawn with pen, ink, and ruler and can also be made with the diagonal and underscore key. *[ ]*

9.61. Square brackets are preferred.

9.62. Brackets are used to enclose your own words within a quotation.
See Term Paper Page 3.

9.63. Brackets are used within a quotation to indicate a correction, personal comment, or an explanation.
See Term Paper Page 7.

9.64. Brackets are used to set off parenthetical expressions within a quotation.
See Term Paper Page 3.

9.65. Brackets are used as parentheses within parentheses.
See Term Paper Page 4.

Parentheses ( )

9.66. Parentheses are used to enclose a thought within a sentence that is part of the contextual matter but not within a quotation.
See Term Paper Pages 4, 7.

9.67. Enclose numerals in parentheses.
Ex: He will (1) run, (2) jump, and (3) dive.

Italics <u>Lincoln</u>

9.68. An underlined word indicates that it is in italics if it appears in a book.
See No. 9.70.

9.69. Do not overuse italics, as this deemphasizes what you are trying to achieve—bring attention to the word.

9.70. Anything that appears in italics in a book, periodical, or other printed matter is underlined, as this is the equivalent of italicizing on the typewriter.

Underlining _____

9.71. Use the underscore key to underline.

9.72. Underlining a word gives added emphasis to it.
See No. 9.69.

9.73. Underline words and spaces such as in a heading.
See Term Paper Page 4.

9.74. To emphasize a word within a quotation, underline the word but indicate what you have done by typing [Italics mine] at the end of the quotation.
See Term Paper Page 8.

9.75. Underline book titles.
See Term Paper Bibliography.

9.76. The repeated use of the underscore key (or holding it down if electric) results in an underlining that separates the text from the footnotes. This line is 15 to 18 spaces in length, but be consistent.
See Nos. 5.16a, 5.17, 9.122 and Term Paper Page 16.

Ellipses . . .   .

9.77. A series of dots with one space between is used to indicate omissions of parts of sentences, entire sentences, and paragraphs.

9.78. Three spaced dots (periods) with a space before and after indicates an omission within a sentence.
See Term Paper Page 9.

9.79. Three spaced dots plus an additional dot for the period indicates an omission at the end of a sentence.
See Term Paper Page 9, No. 9.80.

9.80. Do not leave a space before the first period described in No. 9.79 above.
See Term Paper Page 9.

9.81. To indicate the omission of an entire line or paragraph, the spaced dots extend from left to right margin.
See Term Paper Page 9.

9.82. If you deliberately omit a line or a paragraph from a poem, the ellipses are only as long as the line of poetry.
See No. 9.59.

Dash —

9.83. A dash is made with two hyphens with no space before or after.
See Term Paper Title Page and Page 12.

9.84. A dash may be used to indicate a forceful ending of a sentence.
See Term Paper Page 12.

Virgule or Slash /

9.85. Use the diagonal key to separate choices such as and/or.
See No. 9.38 line two.

Period .

9.86. Leave two spaces after a period when it ends a sentence.

9.87. Leave one space after a period when it is used to separate initials in a person's name.
See Term Paper Page 6.

9.88. Periods usually go inside quotation marks.
See Term Paper Page 10.

Comma ,

9.89. Commas go inside quotation marks.
See Term Paper Page 7.

9.90. Commas are used in words in a series.
See Term Paper Page 14.

9.91. Commas are used to enclose (a) parenthetical expressions and (b) words in apposition. A parenthetical expression is a word or words that could be omitted from a sentence without changing its meaning.
See Term Paper Pages 4, 7, 10, and 13.

An appositive is a word or phrase that explains or identifies something that immediately precedes it.
See Term Paper Pages 7, 8, 11.

Exclamation Point !

9.92. If an older typewriter does not have an exclamation point, it can be made by using the period and the apostrophe keys.

9.93. Leave two spaces after the exclamation point when it ends a sentence.
See Term Paper Page 11.

9.94. The exclamation point used at the end of a sentence can indicate irony, excitement, and/or emotion.
See Term Paper Page 11.

9.95. If the exclamation point is part of the quotation, it goes inside the quotation.
See Term Paper Page 6.

Hyphen -

9.96. The hyphen is typed with no space before or after it.
See Term Paper Page 4.

9.97. Word divisions are made with the hyphen. Avoid word divisions.

9.98. Compound words and compound numbers require a hyphen.
See Term Paper Page 3.

9.99. A hyphen is used to separate two words that might otherwise be confusing.
Ex: Eight foot-soldiers were given decorations.

Double Quotation Marks " "

9.100. Quotation marks (double) are used to enclose a short quotation.
See Term Paper Page 10.

9.101. Slang words are enclosed in quotation marks.
See Term Paper Page 3.

9.102. Titles of periodicals and parts of larger works (books) are enclosed in quotation marks.
See Term Paper Bibliography. See No. 4.29.

Single Quotation Marks ‘ ’

9.103. A quote within a quotation is set off with single quotation marks.
See No. 9.132.

Colon :

9.104. Leave two spaces after a colon when the next word starts with a capital letter.

9.105. Separate time and ratios with colons.
Ex: 8:23 p.m.
She has a 2:1 chance of winning.

9.106. If the main thought is followed by a second independent thought, end the main thought with a colon.

9.107. The colon goes outside the quotation mark.

Semicolon ;

9.108. Leave one space after the semicolon.
See Term Paper Page 7.

9.109. If there are two main thoughts within a sentence and they are not joined by a conjunction, use a semicolon.
See Term Paper Page 13.

9.110. The semicolon goes outside the quotation mark.

Question Mark ?

9.111. Question marks go inside a direct quotation if part of the quote.

9.112. A question mark ends a direct question.
See Term Paper Page 16.

9.113. A question mark used within a sentence may indicate uncertainty, irony, or scorn.
See Term Paper Page 8.

Footnotes

9.114. There are seven component parts to a footnote.
        See No. 4.11.

9.115. When you type something in your paper that will have a foot-
        note, indicate this by typing a raised (superior) number slightly
        above the line and at the end of the passage where a punctua-
        tion mark (except a dash) appears. The superior or footnote
        number comes *before* the dash. Place the footnote on the same
        page as the reference cited.
        See Term Paper Page 16, No. 5.13.

9.116. Type footnotes on a separate sheet of paper to determine space
        needs. Then you will know where your last line of type on the
        page will be so that you can leave enough lines for your foot-
        notes(s).
        See Nos. 8.18, 8.25, 9.24–.25.

9.117. Here is how you determine how much space is needed for a
        footnote:
        Immediately after typing the superior number, roll your pa-
        per down to the bottom margin. Look at the number of lines
        the footnote requires, which you have typed on a separate
        sheet of paper. If the footnote requires two lines (single-
        spaced!), then you will need a total of four single spaces for
        your first footnote as shown in the example below. A page
        with *two* footnotes requires eight lines if each footnote is two
        lines long.
        Ex: *(See No. 5.18)*

Lines	that is, except the Secretary of War!
1	
2	_____
3	
4	[15] The true date was Saturday, April 15. <u>New York</u>
	<u>Herald</u>,
5	Whole No. 10,456.
6	
7	[16] <u>New York Herald</u>, Saturday, April 15, 1865, p. 1,
8	col. 4, lines 28–30.

9.118. To avoid having an overcrowded page and inadequate room for footnotes, look ahead to the next footnote to be typed. Notice the amount of space it requires. Then you will know if you have room for that footnote or whether you should plan your page so that the superior number for it appears at the top of the next page with its accompanying footnote at the bottom.

9.119. If your footnote is so long that not all of it can fit on one page, here is what you do:

   a. Begin typing the footnote as usual and stop at the end of the line. Be sure to break your footnote somewhere within the sentence. Do not type "continued on next page."

   b. Go to the next page and type a solid line of underscores from left to right margin one line below your last line of type.

   c. Double-space below this line and continue typing the footnote.

   d. If appropriate, continue additional footnotes on the page. *See No. 5.11.*

9.120. Although it is possible to complete a footnote at the bottom of the next page (See No. 9.119), it is better to retype the page and get the complete footnote on the page where it really belongs.

9.121. Indent the first line of the footnote seven spaces and begin typing. Type succeeding lines in the same footnote flush with the left margin.
   See Nos. 4.12 F.

9.122. Separate the last line of text on a page that has footnotes with one or two blank lines but be consistent. Type your underlining and then the footnotes.
   See Nos. 5.16 a, 5.17, 9.76, Term Paper Page 8.

9.123. Footnotes are commonly numbered consecutively throughout the paper.
   See Term Paper.

9.124. There are four acceptable methods for numbering footnotes.
   See No. 5.9.

9.125. A footnote is preceded by a raised (superior) number. This number is the same one used in the context on the page you are citing.
See Term Paper Page 13, Nos. 5.12–.13.

9.126. Footnotes must be double-checked for accuracy, because the reader may want to read the exact reference you have cited.

9.127. A footnote may appear in a shortened form when the same reference has already been cited in your paper. Notice the full reference to Eisenschiml's book on Term Paper Page 3 and then see the shortened form on page 8.

9.128. If the last page of your paper contains only a few lines and requires a footnote, here is what you do:
Finish typing the paper. Then, space down to the bottom margin and space up the number of spaces needed for your footnote plus two additional spaces. Type your underlining. Double-space and type your footnote.

9.129. If using in-text documentation with endnotes, type "Notes" or "Works Cited" two inches (twelve vertical lines) from the top edge of the paper, enclose in quotation marks, and center. Space down four single lines from the heading to begin typing the citations. Use single or double spacing.
See Nos. 5.33–.35, 5.44–.46.

Quotations

9.130. A long quotation (more than three lines) appears in block, single-spaced, indented 5 spaces on left and right margins, and does not have quotation marks.
See Term Paper Pages 3, 12.

9.131. If blocked quotations are more than one paragraph in length, double-space between paragraphs.

9.132. If you include a quotation within a quotation, the inside quotation has single quotation marks while the outside quotation has double quotation marks. This rule applies only when quotations appear in a sentence of double-spaced text rather than as a separate paragraph.

9.133. Short quotations are double-spaced and run into the contextual matter.
See Term Paper Page 2.

Bibliography

9.134. The bibliography has six component parts.
See No. 4.11.

9.135. The bibliography constitutes the last page of your paper. Use single spacing but double-space between entries. Put page number at bottom.
See Term Paper Bibliography.

9.136. The bibliography contains only references actually used in the paper. It does not include references read but discarded such as may be in your working bibliography.
See Nos. 4.1–.2, 4.6.

9.137. Type the word Bibliography in capital letters at top center, leaving a three-inch top margin and type on line 18. Do not underline Bibliography.
See Term Paper Bibliography.

9.138. Arrange the bibliography in alphabetical order.
See Term Paper Bibliography.

9.139. Do not number your bibliographic references.
See Term Paper Bibliography.

9.140. Begin each first line of the references flush with the left margin. Indent remaining lines seven spaces.
See No. 4.12 B and Term Paper Bibliography.

9.141. Double space between each reference.
See Term Paper Bibliography.

AFTER TYPING THE PAPER

9.142. After completing the paper and before submitting it to your instructor, take a few minutes to give it a final inspection by using the term paper checklist shown in Appendix C.

9.143. If your final copy contains a typing error on any page, decide how it will be corrected.
   See Nos. 9.20–.23.

9.144. It is better to retype a page than to make corrections in ink.

9.145. Proofread each page before removing it from the typewriter as this will eliminate the need to realign.

9.146. If you submit your paper in loose form, without staples or clips, type your name (last name first) in the upper right corner of each page, followed by the page number if not already there. Avoid submitting your paper in this form.
   See No. 8.53.

9.147. If you submit your paper in a cover or folder, be sure you have a typed label on the outside with your name and title of the paper on it.
   See Nos. 8.54, 9.40.

10

ORGANIZING FOR WORD PROCESSING

You need to decide on the most appropriate method for producing your term paper. Handwritten papers are almost a thing of the past; typed papers are what most students hand in to their instructors. However, you may be considering a word processor as the medium for getting your paper prepared in its final form. After reading this chapter, you will have a good idea as to which finished paper you wish—the typed paper or the paper prepared on a word processor. Discuss this with your instructor.

A FEW BASIC FACTS

10.1. A computer and a word processor can help you produce a term paper with minimum effort and time *if you know word processing and are comfortable using it*. If not, do not attempt to learn how to use a word processor and prepare a term paper at the same time for this will bring you nothing but frustration, grief, and false starts.

10.2. Having your paper done on a word processor by an experienced operator is quite another matter and worthy of your consideration. Read all items in this chapter and you will know what to do.
See Nos. 10.30–.45.

10.3. Becoming familiar and skilled on a word processor requires a commitment of time, money, and a willingness to learn. If you have a term paper assignment, consider having a skilled operator prepare the finished copy, unless of course, you possess word-processing skills. Look in the Yellow Pages under Word Processing—Services.
See Nos. 10.30–.45.

10.4. Many skilled writers prefer using a typewriter rather than a word processor to prepare copy. In fact, some of our most prominent writers use an office-style manual typewriter rather than a modern electric or electronic typewriter. They want to feel at ease on the typewriter they use and so should you.

WHAT IS WORD PROCESSING?

10.5. Word processing is a term used to describe one of many functions a personal computer can perform. Personal means a small desk-top size rather than the giant type used in large business firms.

10.6. The word processor monitor, like a television screen, displays the information typed on the keyboard or provided in the software or computer memory. Software refers to the "program" on the disk that gives instructions to the machine and operator.

10.7. The software is a "floppy disk" measuring 5½ inches in diameter. It is inserted into a slot on the word-processing machine. The disk contains instructions to the operator who performs a variety of functions by tapping special keys.

10.8. The disk also records information and instructions. Upon command (tapping one or more special keys) the operator input is viewed on the screen for review and editing before it is sent to the printer for typing.
    See No. 10.11.

10.9. The software provides internal instructions to the machine operator (typist) who taps keys by following directions on the screen and entering the information requested.

10.10. The printer (a separate machine but attached by cable to the computer and adjacent to it) transfers the information from the video screen to a typed page upon command of the operator and it does it much faster than a person can type.

10.11. The word processor keyboard has the same keys as a typewriter plus special keys to enable the operator to give commands to the machine. Common commands include "display," "delete," "center," and "underline."

ADVANTAGES OF USING A WORD PROCESSOR

10.12. As with many machines, models may be basic or deluxe. All have distinctive and unique features and functions:

   a. Random Access Memory (RAM) activates upon operator command when certain special keys are tapped.
   b. Read-Only Memory (ROM) is controlled by the computer and acts independently of the operator.
   c. Both RAM and ROM give the computer many functions the typewriter cannot perform.
   d. Some electric and electronic typewriters have some of the features found on the word processor.
      See No. 9.1.
   e. Some word processors have a built-in spelling program that alerts the operator when a word has been misspelled.
   f. Word processors can center headings and titles automatically, keep track of page numbers, and display a complete page or an entire text before it appears in typed form.
   g. Left- and right-hand margins can be made even.
   h. Words and phrases can be underlined automatically.
   i. Print styles and sizes can be changed without effort.
   j. Changes and corrections can be made easily because they appear on the video screen before being typed.

10.13. Your task of preparing your draft and final copy is simplified if you use a word processor because:

   a. You view your writing on a screen and can make changes before they appear in type. This is referred to as editing capability.
   b. The speed in making changes and typing a page far surpasses the speed of a typewriter.
   c. A word, sentence, paragraph, or an entire page can be viewed with ease by simply tapping one or more special keys.
   d. Deleting parts of the paper becomes an easy task by using a special "delete" key.
   e. Erasers, white-out, and correcting tape are not needed.

f. A year's worth of information can be placed on one or two disks, thus eliminating the need for cumbersome files.

g. Expert typing is not needed (the screen displays before putting it on paper) but good proofreading skills are essential.

h. The word processor can produce an attractive paper if the operator is skilled in word processing and uses the software correctly.

i. The special features save time and may even turn your writing task from a chore to fun.

LIMITATIONS AND DISADVANTAGES OF USING A WORD PROCESSOR

10.14. Some word processors have difficulty with or are unable to type footnotes because of their inability to place the footnote number one-half space above the line. It is not possible for the word processor to manually place a number one-half space above a line, unless this ability has been built into the software program.

See No. 9.115.

10.15. The two best reasons for not using a word processor are money and time to learn how to use it.

10.16. The purchase of a word processor and a suitable program designed to perform specific tasks can cost several thousands of dollars.

10.17. Becoming proficient on a word processor is not an easy task and requires many hours of instruction and practice. A new machine, a "personal writer," is much simpler to operate and has many of the word processing functions.

10.18. More than 200 programs are available but unless a program is specifically designed for term papers or research papers, it will be of little help.

10.19. A new electronic or electric typewriter can perform some of the same functions and tasks of a word processor and is far less expensive and easier to use.

See No. 9.1.

10.20. Not all computers are good word processors. Some computers are better suited for video games than for serious writing.

10.21. It is possible to delete an entire page or entire text *accidentally.*

10.22. Disks are not indestructible! If damaged, they may be useless and all the work recorded on them is lost, not retrievable, and must be redone.

10.23. Some word processors divide words unconventionally. Any place in the word may be fair game for dividing. Avoid violating word-division rules.

10.24. If you can't type, consider using the services of a company that specializes in typing term papers and research papers. Look for them in the Yellow Pages under Typing Services and Word Processing Services.
    See Chapter 1, Pages 3–4 (Plagiarism).

10.25. The readability of your completed paper is very important. Letter-quality rather than dot-matrix print is definitely preferred by your instructor.
    See Nos. 10.27–.29 and .46.

10.26. The instruction manual that accompanies the software may be lengthy, technical, and detailed. Time, patience, and practice may be necessary to fully understand and benefit from it.

SAMPLES OF DOT MATRIX, NEAR-LETTER-QUALITY, AND LETTER-QUALITY PRINT

10.27 This is an example of basic dot matrix print. As you can see, it is somewhat difficult to read, and is not acceptable for term papers or other schoolwork. Be sure to ask your instructor whether dot matrix print is acceptable before you print your paper.

10.28 This is an example of near-letter-quality print. It is called near-letter-quality because it closely resembles the type of print found in typewriters and letter-quality printers. This is usually acceptable for term papers and other schoolwork.

10.29 This is an example of letter-quality type print. It is the type of print available from a typewriter or letter-quality printer. Letter-quality print is the easiest to read because it is clear and sharp, not made up of tiny dots. Letter-quality is the preferred type of print for your term paper.

QUESTIONS TO ASK BEFORE USING A WORD PROCESSOR

10.30. Do I have my instructor's approval for submitting a paper done on a word processor?

10.31. If someone will prepare my paper on a word processor, how much time will that person require? This will influence my own timetable for completing the draft I will give to the operator.

10.32. If someone is going to do my paper on a word processor, does that person want to discuss the paper with me before I begin to write?

10.33. What help, if any, is the word-processing operator able to give me concerning how the paper is to be submitted for processing?

10.34. Will I be able to make last-minute changes after giving my paper to the word-processing operator?

10.35. Will the word-processing operator produce my paper using 10-point type and will it be letter-quality?
See Nos. 10.27–.29 and .46.

10.36. Do the word-processing operator and I have an understanding and agreement about the style and format of footnotes, endnotes, and in-text documention?
See Chapters 4 and 5.

10.37. Is my handwriting legible, so the word-processing operator will have no difficulty reading it?

10.38. Does the word-processing operator or service provide editorial assistance or does it merely type what is given without comment or changes?

10.39. Is the burden of proofreading the final copy before it is printed resting with me or with the word-processing operator?

10.40. What is the cost of each page of typed material?

10.41. What is the cost of typing tables, charts, maps, graphs, and other special inclusions?

10.42. Will the word-processing operator be able to include tables, charts, maps, and graphs, or is it beyond the capability of the machine?

10.43. If my draft contains items in color, will the word processor be able to reproduce them?

10.44. Is there a charge for making revisions in my processed draft prepared by the operator?

10.45. May I see a page of what you have typically produced on a word processor so I can examine its appearance and readability?

THE COMPLETED PAPER

10.46. The next page shows how Page 3 of the sample Term Paper could look if a "top of the line" word processor is used. Note that the type is letter-quality. The general appearance of the page is excellent and its readability equals or excels that of a typewritten page.

10.47. Decide whether you wish to have your completed term paper done on a word processor or on a typewriter. If you choose a word processor, review this chapter; if your choice is to have it typewritten, review Chapter 9. Retain a copy in case the original is lost.

his post without proper authority.[2] As shocking as this may be, even more shocking is that protective measures to guard the life of Lincoln were criminally negligent. In addition, the armed guard (Parker) whom Mrs. Lincoln had requested and whose duty it was to stand outside the presidential box and "screen" all passersby, was mysteriously absent from his post at the time Booth made his fateful entry. Also, no one had bothered to notice the peephole in the door that Booth had bored on the morning of the murder. Finally, the broken lock on the door of the presidential box had not been repaired. Into all these errors, omissions, and faulty security measures did the President of the United States walk.

> On the night of April 14, 1865, he [Lincoln] attended a
> performance of Our American Cousin at Ford's Theatre in
> Washington. A few minutes after 10 o'clock [in the evening], a
> shot rang through the crowded house. John Wilkes Booth, one of
> the best-known actors of the day, had shot the President in the
> head from the back of the Presidential box.[3]

Imagine the bedlam, the shrieks, the shouting of the crowd, the general milling of bodies that must have taken place when the audience suddenly realized that something was very wrong! It almost seemed that the crime that had just occurred was of such magnitude that it was incomprehensible.

This tragedy gave rise to even more tragedies as will be explained in this paper. Dr. Samuel Mudd and Mrs. Mary Surrat, for example, were entangled in President Lincoln's murder and each paid dearly for their alleged involvement.

---

[2]Otto Eisenschiml, Why Was Lincoln Murdered? (New York: Grosset and Dunlap, 1937), pp. 12, 14.

[3]The World Book Encyclopedia, 1982 ed., s.v. Lincoln 12:285-6.

11

DEVELOPING THE ORAL REPORT

THE PURPOSE OF THIS CHAPTER

This chapter explains how to give an oral report. For reasons of simplicity, the terms oral report, speech, talk, and presentation are used interchangeably even though differences exist. For example, an oral report is the least formal of the three mentioned. A speech is an expression of thoughts in spoken words with little audience participation. A presentation is usually lengthy (one hour or more) and frequently involves the use of audiovisual aids, demonstrations, and audience participation. The key ideas in this chapter should help you prepare and give a short talk, speech, oral report, or presentation. **Before giving your talk, evaluate it by using the Oral Report Checklist shown in Appendix A.**

ORAL REPORTING IS AN IMPORTANT SKILL

11.1. It is important for you to be able to speak to groups of people because you will have to do that in whatever career you choose.

11.2. If you can speak effectively before an audience, large or small, your oral communication skills will help you advance in your career.

11.3. Good oral communication skills are in great demand; they are also poorly developed.

DIFFERENCES BETWEEN THE TERM PAPER AND THE ORAL REPORT

11.4. The term paper and the oral report have important differences:
- A term paper transmits the message by written or typed words. It is read by someone without your being persent.

Interaction is delayed and when it occurs involves only the reader and the writer.

- An oral report is given to a "live" audience. Interaction is immediate. Rather than one receiver, there may be several or hundreds. Your voice is the communication medium.

11.5. Unlike the term paper, your audience will not know if you can spell the words you are using. Most likely, they *will* know if you are pronouncing them correctly. Grammar, word usage, organization, preparation, and rehearsal are still essential.

WHY GIVE A SPEECH?

11.6. Every speech must have a purpose or there is no reason to give it.

11.7. A speech is usually given to persuade, motivate, instruct, inform, discuss, and recognize (national holiday, important event, etc.).

11.8. Oral reports are given when it is believed that talking to an audience is a better way of transmitting a message than by submitting a written or typed report to be read at a later date and without an immediate exchange of ideas between the sender and the receiver.

WHY SPEECHES FAIL

11.9. Speeches fail because they are poorly organized and lack adequate rehearsal. If you hear a speaker make such statements as "Oh, that reminds me . . ." or "I forgot to mention . . . ," it indicates a weakness in organization and rehearsal effort.

SELECT A TOPIC WITH CARE

11.10. You may be assigned a topic or may have the option of choosing one.
See Chapter 2.

11.11. If you choose a topic, select one that is not offensive, in good taste, worthy of your time, and makes a positive contribution to the audience.
See Chapter 2.

11.12. Select a topic familiar to you to reduce the time you will need to collect your data.
See Chapter 2.

11.13. If your topic is noncontroversial, use a direct approach. Here, you first explain your point of view, follow with facts, provide a rationale, and conclude with a summary.

11.14. If your topic is controversial, organize your speech by beginning with facts, followed by a rationale, and concluding with your value judgments and/or recommendations, if appropriate.
See No. 11.96.

11.15. It is better to discuss only one or two points in a speech than to try to cover the entire topic.

HOW MUCH SHOULD A SPEAKER KNOW ABOUT THE TOPIC?

11.16. A good speaker should be as knowledgeable as possible about the topic. This does not mean one is expected to know all there is to know about the subject to be discussed. There are many subjects about which little is known; however, these topics can still be developed into oral reports with some research effort.

11.17. The most difficult thing to do when given an assignment is to get started. Do not procrastinate.

11.18. Establish target dates for the following:

Chapter Reference	*Month*	*Day*	
11.10–.15.	_____	_____	Identify the topic
11.16.	_____	_____	Write a clear statement of the purpose of the talk
11.21–.26.	_____	_____	Research the topic
11.27–.28.	_____	_____	Develop an outline
11.33–.39.	_____	_____	Write the draft
11.40.	_____	_____	Edit and type the draft
11.41–.47.	_____	_____	Edit and type the *final* copy

11.64–.65. _____ _____ Rehearse the oral report
11.84–.116. _____ _____ Give the oral report

11.19. The following flow chart should help you complete your assignment:

Choose a topic
⬇
Analyze the audience
⬇
Gather the data
⬇
Prepare your outline
⬇
Write the draft
⬇
Edit your draft
⬇
Type your second draft or final copy
⬇
Tape your edited final copy
⬇
Decide whether to read your speech or use note cards
⬇
Rehearse your oral report
⬇
Visit the room where you will give your talk
⬇
Determine your equipment needs
⬇
Decide on audio-visuals and demonstrations
⬇
Give your presentation

ANALYZE THE AUDIENCE

11.20. Try to get the answers to these important questions:
  • Who is my audience?
  • How much do they know about the topic?
  • If they do not have much knowledge about the topic, what words shall I use that will clearly express my thoughts (avoiding difficult and technical terms)?

- If they have expressed an opinion about the topic, what is it?
- Why should the audience be interested in my topic? (A vested interest, perhaps? If so, discover what it is!)
- What is the size of the group? (Large, small, etc.)
- What is their age range? (16–18; 25–60, etc.)
- What are their attitudes about the topic? Friendly?
- Hostile? Apathetic? Empathetic?
- What will be the mix of males and females?
- What is the audience's educational level? (high school, etc.)
- What effect do I want my talk to have on the audience?
- What strategy will I need to follow to accomplish the purpose of my talk?
- Will a question-and-answer period be appropriate?

See No. 2.8.

GATHER YOUR DATA

11.21. Review Chapters 3 and 6 on using the library and taking notes.

11.22. Collect more data than you need. This will help you if you have a question and answer period following your talk.
See Nos. 11.111–.116.

11.23. Use 3- by 5-inch index cards or paper cut to size to collect your data, holding them horizontally.
See Nos. 6.5–.7.

11.24. Place only one fact on each card or paper, using one side only. If you need more writing space, go to a second card or paper and use a numbering system to link both such as 1A, 1B.

11.25. Use the reverse side to cite the data source in case you need to verify some fact.
See No. 6.2.

11.26. Save all note cards for possible future referral.

PREPARE YOUR OUTLINE

11.27. Prepare an outline from your note cards by arranging them in some logical order.
See Chapter 7.

11.28. The arrangement of your outline is determined by the strategy you will use in presenting your topic to the audience.
See Nos. 11.20, 11.29–.32.

THE TYPICAL SPEECH HAS THREE PARTS

11.29. Speeches usually include introductory comments that set the theme for the talk, followed by the body where the main points are developed, and conclude with a summary and/or recommendations, if appropriate.

THE OPENING AND CLOSING SHOULD BE DYNAMIC

11.30. Your opening remarks need to gain immediate audience attention; otherwise, they will listen for a short while and then turn their attention elsewhere. A good way to attract attention is to ask a question or display some object for their viewing.

11.31. Gain the audience's attention but avoid startling dramatics that may frighten or alarm them.

11.32. The opening and closing must support each other and both must capture the interest of the audience.

WRITE THE DRAFT

11.33. Be generous in your use of action verbs for they are more interesting than are the passive type.
See Nos. 8.1, 8.3, 8.6, 8.27–.34, 8.37.

11.34. Avoid passive verbs. (Example: "It is appreciated . . ."—Say, "I appreciate . . .")

11.35. The simple sentence having a subject, verb, and object is easy to write and easy to understand.

11.36. Use adjectives and adverbs carefully, as they may be interpreted differently.

11.37. Give special attention to grammar, sentence structure, and transitional devices. (Examples of transitions: "On the other hand . . .", "My second point is . . .", "But . . .") Transitions help achieve forward movement by keeping your audience with you on the point you are discussing.

11.38. Avoid unnecessary words. (Example: "I would like to take this opportunity to thank you for . . ." when "Thank you for . . ." is more to the point.)

11.39. Use paragraph headings and underline them. When reading a typed speech from 8½- by 11-inch white paper, the paragraph headings may be all you need to discuss the content of the paragraph without having to read every word.
See Term Paper Page 2, No. 9.52.

EDIT YOUR DRAFT

11.40. After putting your draft aside for a day or two, edit it. In the editing process, you will do some or all of the following:
- Underline words you want to emphasize.
- Write reminders to yourself at appropriate places. (Examples: Pause here, look at audience, display object.)
- Delete Latin terms and trite expressions. (Examples: *modus operandi,* "Be that as it may.") They are not always understood, nor appreciated.
- Avoid slang expressions.
- Refrain from using words that may convey different meanings. (Examples: *bread*—money, food; *pad*—writing tablet, bed.)
- Eliminate duplication of thoughts.
- Reduce the use of "which" and "that."
- Maintain an average sentence length of 15–19 words.
- Avoid sexist language (Example: "The manager spoke to *his* staff.") Some managers are women!
- Put people into your speech by using names.
- Avoid stilted and impersonal language. (Example: "It behooves me to say . . ." and "It has been said . . ." when "I would like to say . . ." and "We often hear it said that . . ." is better.)
See No. 8.31.

TYPE YOUR SECOND DRAFT OR FINAL COPY

11.41. Review Chapter 9, especially Nos. 9.13, 9.14, 9.16–.19.

11.42. Use the largest type size available. If only elite or pica size is available, type the speech using all capital letters for easy reading.
See No. 9.16.

11.43. Have 1½-inch left and right margins.

11.44. Have one-inch top and bottom margins.

11.45. Triple-space throughout but leave four single spaces between paragraphs.

11.46. Type page numbers on all pages.
See No. 9.35–.37.

11.47. Try to end a paragraph on a page rather than continuing onto another page and thus avoid the need to carry over a thought.

TAPE YOUR EDITED FINAL COPY

11.48. After your speech has been edited, dictate it into a tape recorder.
See No. 11.49 before doing this.

11.49. Speak at about 120 words a minute. Here is how you can do this:
> With your typed speech in front of you, mark off 30 words and place a diagonal mark at that place; do the same after every 30 words. Now, using a watch with a second hand, begin dictating (practice first) your speech to arrive at the first diagonal in 15 seconds. Continue dictating to arrive at the second diagonal mark in another 15 seconds. Do the same for each group of 30 words. At this rate, you will be speaking at 120 words a minute. Note this example of inserting diagonal marks:

LINCOLN'S ASSASSINATION—A MURDER MYSTERY

    The purpose of this presentation is to point out some of the mysteries surrounding the tragic death of President Abraham Lincoln. The murder of this great man is considered to/be one of the greatest tragedies befalling the American people. Another tragedy stemming from the murder is the apparent breakdown of jurisprudence which took place following the killing. With each/passing year, the murder plot and subsequent assassination become more dimmed and the circumstances of the conspiracy, the act itself, and the trial are now hidden among a maze of/abstractions and generalities with each writer's interpretation of the tragedy connected with the President.

This marking method will also help you estimate with some accuracy the length of your talk. Determine the total number of words in your speech and divide by 120. If your speech, for example, contains 1,200 words, and you speak at 120 words a minute, your speech is 10 minutes long.

11.50. Now that you know the length of your talk, in its present form, you may have to shorten or lengthen it to keep within the time allowance given you. If shortening is needed, look for ways of removing parts of your speech that may be interesting but not necessary. If lengthening is needed, go back to your research note cards. See Nos. 6.5, 11.26. Look for additional data you have not used and see where it might be inserted into your talk.

11.51. With your final edited copy before you, repeat No. 11.48.

11.52. Listen to the tape recording, paying close attention to diction, pronunciations, voice emphasis, tonal qualities, and speed. The way you use your voice (strategic pauses and higher and lower tones) provides the punctuation for your speech.

11.53. Pronounce all word endings and syllables. (Examples: say "swimming" instead of "swimmin"; say "particu*lar*ly" instead of "particuly.")

11.54. Avoid regional accents. Emulate news commentators you hear on the radio and TV, for their speech is free of regional accents. A listener usually cannot get a clue as to their country of origin or where they call "home" in the United States.

11.55. Determine if there is a sincere and confident quality to your speech. Does it sound like you? Does it carry conviction?

11.56. If you have stumbled over the pronunciations of words, substitute easier ones. A thesaurus will help.

11.57. Have someone listen to your tape and evaluate it.

11.58. As you listen to the tape, follow along in your typed speech and underline words you want to emphasize.

DECIDE WHETHER TO READ YOUR SPEECH OR USE NOTE CARDS

11.59. Do not attempt to memorize your speech. The most experienced speakers are sometimes at a loss for words because of a memory gap.

11.60. If you are a novice at giving speeches, follow the advice of professional speakers. They recommend that you read your speech, making sure it is done in a way that maintains interest and eye-to-eye contact with the audience.

11.61. Whether you plan to read your speech or use note cards, rehearse, rehearse, rehearse!
    See No. 11.64.

11.62. If you decide to use note cards, use either the 3- by 5- or 5- by 8-inch size. Print the key ideas using a black felt marking pen. Do not use complete sentences. Print is more legible than handwriting. Hold the cards vertically.

11.63. Number each card in the upper right-hand corner. Staple all cards in the upper left corner. If the cards are accidentally dropped during your talk, they can be recovered without having to be put back into their proper order. Do the same if using a typed speech.

REHEARSE YOUR ORAL REPORT

11.64. Get enthused about giving your talk. Getting "psyched up" helps reduce tension, stress, and anxiety concerning your attitudes toward your talk. Consider this:

- You have researched your topic.
- You know more about your topic than does the audience.
- You are prepared to answer questions because you have collected more data than you need.
- You have rehearsed so much that you are completely familiar with your speech.

11.65. When you rehearse, do all of the following:

- Have an audience even if it is only a vacant chair or one person.
- Stand in front of a full-length mirror to observe your body movements (keep them to a minimum).
- Have a platform for your typed speech or note cards (table, stack of books, box, etc.).
- Keep one finger on the line of your typed speech as you read it to avoid losing your place.
- Look at your audience as much as possible.
- Use a pleasant, nonthreatening voice with strategic pauses, proper emphasis, and changes in speed.
- Rehearse enough times to become thoroughly acquainted with your speech and thus increase your ability to maintain eye contact with the audience.

VISIT THE ROOM WHERE YOU WILL GIVE YOUR TALK

11.66. The physical setting where you will give your talk is important and you should visit it and make note of the following:

- Does the room have windows? Try to get a room with windows and chairs that face *away* from the outside light.
- Where are the wall electrical outlets located? Are they where you need them if using equipment powered by electricity (slide or film projector)?
- Can the outlets receive a three-prong plug? If not, you will probably need an adapter as most electrically operated viewing machines have a three-prong plug. A hardware store sells adapters.
- What are the seating arrangements? Are they tablet-arm chairs? Auditorium type seats? Are the seats fixed or mov-

able? Are they facing the direction you desire? Will someone rearrange them for you if you wish?

- Are the windows equipped with curtains or shades? Do the
windows open? Do the curtains and shades work?
- What instructional (audiovisuals, chalkboard, easel, etc.)
equipment is in the room? Does the room have a screen for
viewing slides or films? Do you know how to operate the
equipment you will use in your presentation? If not, have
someone instruct you.
- Does the room have light switches? Where, and how many?
Is it possible to turn off *some* but not *all* of the lights?
(Avoid showing an image on a screen in total darkness because people cannot take notes, and might trip over electrical wires or people if they do not remain in their chairs.)
- Will there be noises or distractions over which you have no
control such as road repairs, building construction? If so,
this may influence the way you want the seats to face or
your choice of room.

DETERMINE YOUR EQUIPMENT NEEDS

11.67. Now that you have visited the room where you will give your
presentation, you know what equipment is available or what
you will need:

(Check what you need)

Chalkboard	_____
Eraser	_____
Chalk	_____
Screen	_____
Easel and pad	_____
Film projector (16 mm?)	_____
Slide projector (carousel type?)	_____
Adapter for a three-prong plug	_____
Lectern equipped with lighting device	_____
Pointer	_____
Microphone	_____
Extension cord	_____
Marking pen (broad felt tip)	_____

11.68. Arrange to have whatever equipment and supplies you need available when you give your presentation, and know how to use them in case the A-V operator is not present.

PREPARE YOUR AUDIOVISUALS AND DEMONSTRATIONS

11.69. When properly used, slides, transparencies, films, drawings, illustrations, chalkboard notes, and easel pad sketches can be effective.

11.70. Avoid freehand drawings. Prepare beforehand, if possible.

11.71. Visuals should be simple, few in number, carefully and accurately made, easy to understand, and large enough for all to see.

11.72. Each visual on a screen should be supported by a prepared text written on an index card.

11.73. Charts are best prepared on one-inch grid paper. A 27- by 32½-inch easel pad sheet (50 sheets to a pad) and marked off in light blue square inches is ideal. The grid allows you to draw straight lines and helps achieve proportional accuracy in charts such as column diagrams and graphs.

11.74. Demonstrations are more effective when there is audience participation. Arrange for a "volunteer" beforehand.

11.75. If using an easel, put penciled notes, lightly printed, on the left side of the easel pad sheet. This is your script and it cannot be seen by the audience and thus frees you from referring to notes that are hand-held.

11.76. A pointer, rather than a finger, is preferred when calling attention to something being projected on a screen or written on an easel pad sheet and does not get in the way of the audience's view.

YOUR APPEARANCE IS IMPORTANT

11.77. Before entering the room where you will give your talk, view yourself in a mirror. Hair combed? Face, hands, and fingernails clean? Tie straight? Trousers arranged properly? Makeup on as it should be?

11.78. Whatever you wear should be clean, without rips or missing buttons.

11.79. Minimize wearing jewelry. A simple necklace, bracelet, earrings, ring, and watch are suitable for female speakers. Male speakers may properly wear a ring and watch. Anything more might distract the audience.

11.80. Avoid being over- or underdressed. If you know the audience, dress appropriately.

YOUR RAPPORT WITH THE AUDIENCE MUST BE POSITIVE

11.81. Avoid trying to flatter your audience. (Examples: "I'm honored to be your speaker" or "I feel humble talking to this group.") It does not sound sincere.

11.82. Never apologize to your audience. (Example: "I haven't had time to properly prepare my talk" or "I'm not the best qualified to speak on this subject" or "A coin was tossed as to who would be your speaker and you got me—sorry about that.")

11.83. Do not end your presentation by thanking the audience. When your presentation has ended, pick up your notes and return to your seat.

GIVE THE PRESENTATION

11.84. If your voice is soft, speak louder than usual.

11.85. If you need to remind yourself to speak to be heard, write the word LOUD on an index card and keep it alongside your notes or typed speech as you address the audience.

11.86. If you use a microphone, speak from 6 to 12 inches away from it. Practice beforehand and learn how to turn it on and off and how to raise and lower it.

11.87. Hold your body movements to a minimum and stand in a relaxed posture.

11.88. Avoid finger pointing and table pounding as a form of emphasis as these are threatening and upsetting gestures.

11.89. Place both hands on the lectern and leave them there.

11.90. Refrain from running your hands through your hair, tossing your hair to keep it out of your eyes (use pins), scratching, rubbing your nose, or clearing your throat, as these are signs of tension and stress.

11.91. Tension and stress are normal and serve to remind speakers to be prepared. Thus, both tension and stress can be viewed as helpful. Adequate rehearsal reduces tension and stress.

11.92. Avoid the use of crude, vulgar, and obscene language.

11.93. If a noise (passing motorist, airplane, etc.) occurs while you are speaking, remain silent until the noise stops. Do not compete with it by shouting to be heard. (This also gives you a little rest break.)

11.94. Observe the audience as you talk. If they look confused about something you have said, rephrase it for better understanding.

11.95. Have a contingency (backup) plan ready in case you are unable to be heard (outside noises) or seen (evening power failure). Plan what to do in such an eventuality.

11.96. If your topic is controversial or one in which you have an unpopular opinion, keep your emotions under control and do not try to *tell* your audience anything. Plan your strategy for getting them to accept your viewpoint.
See No. 11.14.

11.97. Be yourself. The audience will know if you are putting on "airs."

11.98. Avoid the common tendency to use such expressions as "You know," "Okay," and "Uh-huh."

11.99. Inform the audience of how long you will speak. If they don't wonder, their attention may not wander!

11.100. To prevent exceeding your time allowance, arrange beforehand for someone in the front row to give you a two-minute warning signal indicating that you have two minutes left in your speech.

11.101. A short talk does not require a rest break—longer ones do. A one-hour presentation (or longer) will generate audience restlessness and a rest break will be needed. Either have them stand for a stretch (without leaving their seating area) or give them a ten-minute break. Letting them leave the room is risky; some people will not return, others will delay their return and arrive back in the room when you are speaking and be a distraction. Use good judgment.

11.102. During your talk, watch the audience for signs of boredom, confusion, inattentiveness, etc. If you feel you are losing their interest, you can regain it by asking direct and indirect questions:

- Direct—(Select someone from the audience). Look at that person and ask a nonthreatening, easy-to-answer question that has some relationship to your immediate statements. (Example: "Alice, if you have heard of the term acid rain, please tell us what that term means to you"—where the subject being discussed deals with pollution.)
- Indirect—(Look at audience but at no one in particular). Ask a question designed to regain their attention. (Example: "What do you think of the idea of finding water with a forked stick?"—where the subject is water dowsing.)

TELLING JOKES AND FUNNY STORIES CAN BE RISKY

11.103. In general, avoid telling jokes and funny stories.

11.104. A joke is appropriate only when it has some relationship to the topic.

11.105. If you plan to tell a joke, do not preface it by saying "This reminds me of a story . . ." Use an opening statement that leads normally into the joke.

11.106. Some stories and jokes are always inappropriate because they are insulting, crude, offensive, and without merit. Use good judgment.

11.107. A serious topic need not be *deadly* serious. Humor, properly used, can keep the speech from being dull. Remember to smile on occasion during your talk unless the subject (topic) makes smiling inappropriate.

11.108. Long presentations should be supported by some change in activity such as looking at an object, asking questions, etc., to maintain interest and reduce audience fatigue.

USE HANDOUT MATERIALS JUDICIOUSLY

11.109. Handout materials, if used, should be few in number, simple in design, and easy to understand.

11.110. Have someone distribute your handout materials and let them know when you want them to do this.

PREPARE FOR A QUESTION-AND-ANSWER PERIOD

11.111. If you know the answer to a question, give a simple, brief response to avoid using up valuable time for other questions.

11.112. Avoid asking questions that can be answered with "Yes" or "No," or "I don't know."
See No. 11.102.

11.113. Reduce the risk of not being able to answer questions by adequately researching your topic.
See Nos. 11.16, 11.22.

11.114. If the audience asks questions, consider it a compliment because it means they have been listening.

11.115. If you don't know the answer to a question, admit it. Don't fake an answer. The most experienced speakers get questions they cannot answer. Either say, "I don't know," or promise to get the answer to them as soon as possible.

11.116. Have several blank index cards with you for writing questions for which you don't have immediate answers. Note who asked the question. Obtain the answer as soon as possible and give it to that person.

KEEP SPEECH, EVALUATE AND REVISE IT

11.117. Retain your typed speech or notes and your research cards; you may be asked to present it to another audience.

11.118. At the top left corner of the first page, indicate the following:
- Date on which you gave the presentation
- The audience (identify by name and city) and number present
- The number of minutes you spoke
- Number of words in your typed speech
- The questions, if any, asked by the audience
- Your own evaluation of the effectiveness of your speech (good, fair)

11.119. While your oral report is fresh in your mind, write suggestions about how it could be improved, if given again.

11.120. Locate the sections in your speech where challenges came from the audience. Review your data to eliminate future challenges.

11.121. Review the Oral Report Checklist in Appendix A and evaluate your speech.

11.122. Use this checklist *before* and *after* your oral presentation.

Appendix A

ORAL REPORT CHECKLIST

Chapter Reference		Yes	No
Appendix C	1. Have I examined the term paper checklist on pages 147–49 as a means of improving the quality of my typed speech (not all items are appropriate)?	___	___
11.59–.63.	2. If speaking from note cards, are my key words underlined and in large print for easy reading?	___	___
11.63.	3. Are my note cards or typed speech numbered and stapled to prevent a "disaster" if they are accidentally dropped during my presentation?	___	___
9.5, 9.16.	4. Have I used a new black ribbon on the typewriter, and are the type bars clean?	___	___
9.7, 9.12.	5. Have I typed on white 8½- by 11-inch paper of heavy weight (20- or 24-pound)?	___	___
11.42–.44.	6. Is my speech typed in all capitals for easy reading?	___	___
11.45.	7. Have I used triple spacing in the body of the speech and left four single lines between paragraphs?	___	___
11.20.	8. Have I analyzed my audience—their interests, points of view, knowledge of the topic, educational level, etc.?	___	___

continued on next page

Chapter Reference		Yes	No

Chapter Reference			Yes	No
11.30.	9.	Does my speech have a definite purpose or message?	___	___
11.13–.15, 11.19–.20, 11.96.	10.	Have I planned my strategy for making an effective presentation?	___	___
11.11, 11.20.	11.	Have I identified what I want my audience to gain from my oral report?	___	___
11.60, 11.65.	12.	Do I maintain good eye contact with my audience?	___	___
11.102.	13.	Do I keep their attention from wandering by asking direct and/or indirect (overhead) questions?	___	___
11.94, 11.102.	14.	Am I watching for signals from my audience such as confusion and, if so, am I prepared to rephrase for better understanding?	___	___
11.117–.122.	15.	Do I feel that my talk will be favorably received?	___	___
11.33–.38, 11.40	16.	During my editing, did I weed out unnecessary words and jargon, and refrain from using words that have unclear meanings?	___	___
11.52, 11.57.	17.	Does my voice sound convincing, interesting, and sincere as I listen to it on the tape recorder?	___	___
11.52.	18.	Do I project my voice in a way to show enthusiasm and confidence?	___	___
11.84–.85.	19.	Is my voice loud enough for all to hear?	___	___
11.30–.32.	20.	Does my opening statement capture the attention of the audience?	___	___
11.31.	21.	Have I waited until I have my audience's attention before speaking?	___	___
11.20.	22.	Is my talk interesting?	___	___
11.30–.32.	23.	Do I begin with an interesting opening, move to the main points, and		

continued on next page

Chapter Reference			Yes	No
		close with a logical conclusion that supports my facts?	___	___
11.49, 11.100.	24.	Can my talk be given within the time allowance set for it?	___	___
11.49.	25.	Am I speaking at about 120 words a minute?	___	___
11.20, 11.64.	26.	Have I done enough research on the topic to be able to handle questions from the audience with ease?	___	___
11.37.	27.	Do I use transitional terms such as "My second point . . .", "On the other hand . . .", and "To summarize . . ." to keep my audience thinking along with me?	___	___
11.61–.62.	28.	Have I rehearsed enough times so that I can give the talk with minimum reliance on my notes or typed speech?	___	___
11.48–.55.	29.	Have I tape-recorded my talk and listened carefully to my voice, word choice, usage, volume, and inflection?	___	___
11.56.	30.	Have I changed words I stumbled over during rehearsal to words that convey the same meaning but are easier to pronounce?	___	___
11.89.	31.	Do I keep my hands motionless and on the lectern?	___	___
11.87–.88.	32.	Do I keep my body movements to a minimum?	___	___
11.90.	33.	Do I refrain from distracting the audience by not picking lint off my clothing, by not clearing my throat, by not rubbing my nose, etc.?	___	___
11.54, 11.98.	34.	Do I use correct grammar and is it free of slang and trite expressions?	___	___
11.77–.80.	35.	Have I checked my appearance in a		

continued on next page

Chapter Reference		Yes	No
	mirror just prior to addressing the audience?	___	___
11.91.	36. Do I appear poised and confident in front of the audience?	___	___
11.107.	37. Do I remember to smile occasionally while I am speaking?	___	___
11.60, 11.65.	38. Do I remember to look around the room as I talk, focusing my eyes first on one person for a while and then on another as a way of keeping their attention and showing interest in them?	___	___
11.68.	39. Am I familiar with the operation of the equipment I plan to use in my presentation?	___	___
11.69–.71.	40. Are my visual aids well made, simple in design, large enough to see, and clearly visible to all in the room?	___	___
11.95.	41. Do I have a contingency (backup) plan ready in case something unexpected happens during my talk (power failure, no lights, etc.)?	___	___

Each of the above questions should be answered with a "Yes." If you have answered "No" to any of them, go back to that particular section of your presentation because it may need improvement.

Appendix B

SAMPLE TERM PAPER

HOW TO USE THIS SAMPLE TERM PAPER

As you will see, the numbers of the key ideas that appear in the text have been noted on the sample term paper. You may easily look up the explanation or the reason for the use of a particular form by turning back from the sample paper to the specific item in the text.

For example, 9.38 on the sample title page of the term paper refers you back to Chapter 9, Item 38 or 9.38.

9.40

Leave twenty-three lines here.

9.38

9.83

LINCOLN'S ASSASSINATION--A MURDER MYSTERY　9.41

Leave three blank lines here ⎯⎯⎯⎯→

by

Leave seven blank lines here ⎯⎯⎯⎯→

Doris Driscoll

8.38

Leave thirteen blank lines here ⎯⎯⎯⎯→

English 100A

Double space　　　　Dr. Michele Kurtz

May 1, 19⎯

9.58

1½ inches

9.42   9.35

LINCOLN'S ASSASSINATION--A MURDER MYSTERY

9.44

The purpose of this paper is to point up some
of the mysteries surrounding the tragic death of
President Abraham Lincoln. The murder of this
great man is considered to be one of the greatest
tragedies befalling the American people. Another
tragedy stemming from the murder is the apparent
breakdown of jurisprudence and American justice
which took place following the killing. With each
passing year, the murder plot and subsequent
assassination become more dimmed, and the
circumstances of the conspiracy, the act itself,
and the trial are now hidden among a maze of
abstractions and generalities with each writer's
interpretation of the tragedy connected with the
President. In fact, a perusal of any number of
books on the subject reveals inconsistencies,
gaps, confusions, and widely differing opinions
of the events leading up to and following the
killing. This term paper will include official
government evidence and will attempt to present
facts rather than fiction about Lincoln's
murder.

It is common knowledge that John Wilkes Booth
killed the President of the United States, but
the part played by those who went on trial for
their lives because they were charged with being
involved in an atrocious crime is still clouded
in a veil of mystery.

This paper will pinpoint certain events
connected with the assassination--events that to **9.83**
this day contribute to the fact that President
Lincoln's assassination is, indeed, a murder
mystery.

9.52 Lincoln's premonition of death

9.53   The years have not divulged the reason why
the President acted so strangely on the day he was
shot. On that particular day, he appeared to be
extremely melancholy. He also expressed the fear
that men were attempting to do him harm. In fact,
when he was leaving the White House to go to
Ford's Theatre, he said "good-bye" rather than
his customary "good night" to his servant. This
attitude of impending disaster and other
statements made by him lead one to wonder from
what source his fears originated. The President
took a fatalistic view of a possible

9.133 assassination. He said, "No use worrying. What
is to be, must be. If anyone is really determined
to kill me, I shall be killed!"[1]

11.39 Lack of adequate protection provided for the
President

It would almost appear that President
Lincoln never had a chance to escape from death
the night of April 14. Four instances will
illustrate this. First, Mrs. Lincoln dismissed
the regular guard and in his place requested that
the President's life be protected by a certain
metropolitan policeman by the name of Parker,
John Parker. It must be assumed that Mrs. Lincoln
did not know that Parker had a reputation for

9.123   [1] Richard N. Current, Mr. Lincoln (New
5.4 York: Dodd, Mead and Co., 1957), p. 382.

drunkenness while on duty. Other charges against
him included conduct unbecoming an officer,
insubordination, and leaving his post without
proper authority.[2] As shocking as this may be,
even more shocking is that protective measures to
guard the life of Lincoln were criminally
negligent. In addition, the armed guard (Parker)   6.29
whom Mrs. Lincoln had requested and whose duty it
was to stand outside the presidential box and
9.101   "screen" all passersby, was mysteriously absent
from his post at the time Booth made his fateful
entry. Also, no one had bothered to notice the
peephole in the door that Booth had bored on the
morning of the murder. Finally, the broken lock
on the door of the presidential box had not been
repaired. Into all these errors, omissions, and
faulty security measures did the President of the
United States walk.

On the night of April 14, 1865, he [Lincoln]   6.28 9.62
9.45   attended a performance of Our American Cousin at
9.130   Ford's Theatre in Washington. A few minutes after
10 o'clock [in the evening], a shot rang through   9.64
the crowded house. John Wilkes Booth, one of the
9.98   best-known actors of the day, had shot the
President in the head from the back of the
Presidential box.[3]

Imagine the bedlam, the shrieks, the
shouting of the crowd, the general milling of
bodies that must have taken place when the
audience suddenly realized that something was
very wrong! It almost seemed that the crime that
had just occurred was of such magnitude that it
was incomprehensible.

5.6 5.8   [2] Otto Eisenschiml, Why Was Lincoln
9.127   Murdered? (New York: Grosset and Dunlap, 1937),   5.7
pp. 12, 14.

5.3b   [3] World Book Encyclopedia, 1982 ed., s.v.
Lincoln 12:285-86.

This tragedy gave rise to even more tragedies as will be explained in this paper. Dr. Samuel Mudd and Mrs. Mary Surrat, for example, were   **9.91a** entangled in President Lincoln's murder and each paid dearly for their alleged involvement.

After shooting Lincoln,⁴ Booth jumped from the presidential box onto the stage. During his leap, he caught the spur of his right boot on the U. S. Treasury flag. This unforeseen accident

9.65 resulted in disaster for Dr. Mudd. (If Booth hadn't broken his leg, he [Mudd] might never have been touched by the tragedy of the President's death.) A small steel ball from Booth's gun changed Samuel Mudd's life.⁵ We will speak more of Dr. Mudd later. Let it suffice to say that tragedy was looming for the Mudd family and they did not know it!

9.73 <u>Booth's change of plans from kidnapping to murder</u>

John Wilkes Booth was a nationally known actor and the grandson of a man who helped runaway slaves escape to freedom. John Wilkes (he often   **6.29** dropped off his family name) was unlike his   **9.66** grandfather in so many ways. Perhaps the biggest difference between the two was that the grandson was a strong southern sympathizer. Kelly makes an interesting statement regarding Booth's motives in the crime when he says:

> Which of the shadows hid the
> demoniacal movements of the man who cast
> himself in the role of the villain in the

5.42 5.1a   ⁴A single-shot, muzzle-loading, .41   **9.96** caliber derringer pistol was used.

5.14 5.1b   ⁵U.S. Department of the Interior, <u>Lincoln Museum and the House Where Lincoln Died,</u> Booklet, reprint (Washington, DC: 1956), p. 14.

5.10
arch tragedy of his own authorship that
night, remains a mystery.[6]

Booth, the idol of the American stage, was a
strange man indeed. His income amounted to over
$20,000 a year, a considerable sum in those days.
He had everything he could possibly want, except
respect. John Wilkes, you see, was not accepted
into "polite" society because of his life
style--questionable and unsavory. There was <u>one</u>
thing he wanted and that, apparently, was undying
fame as the executioner of a "tyrant," for that
is how he viewed Abraham Lincoln.

This attitude which he had toward the
President may help explain why plans to kidnap
the chief executive officer of the nation were
shelved. His plans took a more ominous turn! As
the Civil War casualties mounted, Booth was
dismayed over the number of Confederate losses.
The extent of these losses may have changed
Booth's mind about the practicality of
kidnapping. In its place, another plan
developed. Murder!

The trial and historical accounts of the
incident have never been clear. Were the people
who were arrested as accomplices actually
guilty? Some were but others were not. Did Booth
inform his fellow conspirators about his change
in plans? Perhaps, or perhaps not!

Booth's decision to kill the President may
have resulted from Lincoln's statement of April
5.17
12, that he (Lincoln) hoped that the freed slaves

5.10
[6] Edward James Kelly, <u>The Crime at Ford's
Theatre</u> (Washington, DC: Government Service,
Inc., Action Publishers, 1944), p. 4.

of Louisiana would be given the right to vote.[7]
Kelly remarked that when Booth heard of this, he
fumed loudly and said, "Now, by God, I'll put him   **6.24**
through!"[8]   **9.95**

General Grant's strange behavior

Now let us consider General Ulysses S. Grant   **9.87**
for a moment. The evening at Ford's Theatre was to
honor Lincoln as well as Grant, the victorious
general who had just won the War Between the
States. Unbeknown to either of them, both men had
been targeted for murder by Booth. Both men   **9.69**
represented all that Booth hated. Both men had
the respect and admiration of a grateful nation.
Both men had to be killed. But Fate intervened!

8.28   The President had asked the general and his
wife to join the presidential party because
Lincoln knew that the crowd wanted to pay honor to
their victorious general. "Earlier in the
morning, General and Mrs. Grant had accepted an
invitation from the President to accompany him
and Mrs. Lincoln to the theatre."[9]

8.28   History has never satisfactorily explained
why the general and his lady suddenly notified
the President on the same afternoon of that
terrible day that they (the Grants) would be
unable to attend the performance. Was it because
they decided on the spur of the moment to visit
their two sons who were at a camp in New Jersey?[10]   **8.26**

5.16a _____

5.42 5.12   [7] During the closing days of the war in
1865.

5.3a   [8] Kelly, The Crime, p. 4.
                 [9] Lincoln Museum and the House Where
Lincoln Died, p. 6.

5.20   [10] Ibid.
5.24 (5)

What was their reason for first accepting and
then rejecting the President's invitation? And
so, quite suddenly, the Grants boarded a train at
Union Station and headed for New Jersey.

8.28   Lincoln invited several other people to
attend in place of the Grants but all declined.
Finally, the President was able to get Miss Clara
9.91b   Harris (a senator's daughter) and her escort,
Major Henry R. Rathbone, to join him and Mrs.
Lincoln in the presidential box. Grant's
behavior and his refusal were indeed strange.
Sixteen months later, during the presidency of
Andrew Johnson, Grant accepted another
invitation to attend a reception at the Executive
9.108   Mansion; he considered such an invitation from
the President to be the same as an order; Grant
always said he never disobeyed an order! Why had
the general not considered Lincoln's invitation
to be an order when he did feel the need to obey
the invitation from President Johnson?
Stanton's famous last words about Lincoln
          The dastardly deed had been done. Booth
9.63   carried out his promise to "put him [Lincoln]   6.28
9.89   through," for on the morning of April 15, the
President died in a house across the street from
the theatre.
          An untold number of accounts quote Edwin
9.91b   Stanton, Secretary of War, as saying, "Now he
belongs to the ages" at the moment of Lincoln's
demise. Yet, it is quite likely that this famous
eulogy was never spoken by Stanton or by anyone
9.66   else. Witnesses present at Lincoln's death (and
there were many people crowded into that little

bedroom) later recount many versions of what
Stanton was supposed to have said:

8.24
>   Now he belongs to the angels
>   Now he belongs to history
>   And now he belongs to the ages
>   Doctor, please lead us in prayer
>   Ah dear friend! there is none now to do
>   me justice; none to tell the world of the
>   anxious hours we have spent together!
>   There lies the most perfect ruler of men
>   the world has ever seen.[11]

Booth's escape into Maryland

9.113
Our hero (?) has escaped! And where did Booth
escape to? He must have been having agonizing
pain and was suffering from the effects of a
broken leg received in his fall from the stage.
His pain must have been excruciating and
unbearable because he veered from his chosen
escape route to seek medical help. That is how Dr.
Mudd got involved.

Booth, considering himself to be a national
hero now that he had rid the country of a
"tyrant," made his escape from the theatre,
mounted a horse that was saddled and waiting for
him, and approached the sentry at the Navy Yard
bridge. One historical account states that Booth
said he was a Maryland planter from "near
Beantown."[12] The sentry, Sergeant Silas T. Cobb,   8.19
violated orders by allowing Booth to pass through
the gate after curfew. Eisenschiml's account of
the incident differs widely from Kelly's:

>   A Sergeant Cobb, who was in charge
>   at the north end of the bridge, had   9.74
>   questioned Booth and, after a brief

9.127
5.8   [11] Eisenschiml, <u>Lincoln Murdered</u>, pp. 482-
          84.

9.122
8.19   [12] Kelly, <u>The Crime</u>, p. 15.

conversation, had let him pass . . .
[Italics mine]

6.27 . . . .
It is characteristic of Booth that
he did not hesitate to give his true name
to the sentinel at the bridge, for, in
the fanatic mind of the assassin, his
act was to be the perfect crime of the
ages, and he the most heroic assassin of
all times![13]

9.81 . . . .
To return to Sergeant Cobb, one can
6.25b understand his decision to let Booth . . . pass
9.78 unconditionally. . . . He [Cobb] had to make his   **6.25a 9.80**
decisions, and he made them according to his best   **9.79**
judgment. On what grounds can it be explained,
however, that having heard Booth's name from his
own lips, this soldier did not give the alarm as
soon as the news of Lincoln's assassination
reached him?[14]

Cobb's failure to mention Booth's passing
through his post was never brought up at the
trial. Strange, indeed, that not one of the
prosecuting officers asked the sergeant why he
did not report it.

Confusion rose to new heights in the hours
immediately following Booth's cowardly act. To
cite one illustration, the New York Herald
carried news dispatches in every edition. In the
rush to get out its first extra on the slaying,
the Herald misdated its paper by carrying the
date Friday, April 14, on its masthead.[15]

Secretary of War Stanton's unexplained silence

A second strange event concerns the actions
of the Secretary of War, Edwin Stanton. Rather

5.3a   [13] Eisenschiml, Lincoln Murdered, pp. 107-
          9.

5.20   [14] Ibid., pp. 108-9.
5.24 (6)

5.15   [15] The true date was Saturday, April 15. New   **5.42**
9.117 York Herald, Whole No. 10,456.

than following the most logical course of action
by releasing the name of the assassin to the
newspapers as soon as possible as an aid in
Booth's apprehension, Stanton withheld the name
until several hours after the crime had been
committed. A news dispatch dated April 15 states

9.100   "some evidence of the guilt of the party who   8.21
attacked the President is in the possession of
the police. "[16] It is a well-known fact that

9.88   because of Booth's notoriety as an actor, his
identity was known to almost all in the theater,
especially to his fellow actors and actresses who
were on the stage when he jumped from the
presidential box, brandished a dirk, and yelled
to the audience "Sic Semper Tyrannis" (Ever Thus
to Tyrants). It appears that everyone knew Booth
had killed the President--everyone, that is,
except the Secretary of War!

The cloud of suspicion over Dr. Samuel Mudd

What was Booth doing during the hours
immediately following the shooting? He had made a
safe escape into Maryland although racked by pain
from his injury. Because the home of Dr. Samuel   9.91b
Mudd, a general practitioner, was on Booth's
escape route, it seems only natural that he would
head there to receive first aid.

Dr. Mudd may have been merely an unfortunate
victim of his apparent innocent acquaintanceship
with Booth. Yes, Dr. Mudd was a southerner. Yes,
Dr. Mudd had met the actor John Wilkes Booth. For
this, the doctor received a life sentence for
giving aid and comfort to Booth. His innocence

---

[16] *New York Herald*, Saturday, April 15,
1865, p. 1, col. 4, lines 28-30.

was established and he was absolved of any
complicity of the crime one hundred years <u>after</u>   9.93
his death! Several years after the trial, Mudd   9.94
was pardoned because of his heroic medical deeds
performed while in a federal prison on the Dry
Tortugas. He had escaped the death penalty
because the military court could not prove that
he was guilty of being an accomplice in the crime.
And yet, he was imprisoned. Consider the
following facts in favor of the physician:

    a) He was a doctor sworn by oath to give
       aid to the injured.

    b) There is considerable doubt that Mudd
       knew of the shooting at Ford's
       Theater when Booth approached him for
       treatment. Lack of rapid
       communications plus the fact that
       Mudd treated Booth only hours after
       the crime had been committed raise
       serious doubts as to Mudd's knowledge
       of what Booth had done.

    c) Booth was wearing a false beard when
       he was attended to by Dr. Mudd, and
       thus masked his identity.

    d) Booth certainly did not intend to
       injure himself at Ford's Theatre. He
       would have no reason, therefore, to
       include Dr. Mudd among his
       accomplices. Booth's arrival at
       Mudd's home for first aid may have
       been nothing more than a coincidence.

<u>Mrs. Surrat's sacrifice</u>

    Booth and his confederates, who actually
wielded pistol and dagger as they attacked
government officials marked for death along with
Lincoln, were obviously guilty. Yet, history has
not clearly established the degree of guilt or
innocence of any of the people who went on trial
and who in some cases forfeited their freedom or
their lives. For example, Dr. Mudd may have been

guilty of knowing Booth. Mary Surrat may have
been found guilty because she had a son who was an
active southern courier and because she operated
a boardinghouse where Booth sometimes visited
her son and other men found guilty of the crime.

9.130
> The trial of Mrs. Surrat, first
> woman to be legally executed in the
> United States, provoked unending
> controversy. Many held her to be
> innocent, few believed her degree of
> guilt warranted hanging, but the
> verdict remained unchanged. [17]

A case of mistaken identity

Perhaps the most intriguing and mystifying
aspect of the trial concerned the establishment
of the identity of John Wilkes Booth from a
photograph. Witnesses to the shooting were asked
to identify the photograph as that of the

9.83   murderer--John Wilkes Booth. This they failed to   9.84
do simply because all through the trial the
picture was of Edwin, John's older brother and
also a famous actor.

> Yet, the photograph of Edwin went
> unnoticed into the files of the trial
> and history has failed to record this
> slip--one of the most tragic mistakes in
> American jurisprudence.[18]

6.27 ....

> Of all the mysteries and problems
> arising out of Lincoln's assassination,
> the enigma of how Edwin's photograph
> came to be substituted for that of his
> brother John Wilkes is one of the most
> intriguing.[19]   5.13

---

[17] Kelly, <u>The Crime</u>, p. 31.

[18] Eisenschiml, <u>Lincoln Murdered</u>, pp.
264-65.

5.20   5.24   [19] Ibid., p. 265.
9.56

<u>Booth's diary and the thirteen missing pages</u>

Let us now turn our attention from the trial
to the diary kept by Booth. He had developed a
habit of recording interesting events of the day
9.125   in a small blank book.[20] After he was killed by
federal troops (some historians say Booth took
his own life rather than be captured; and still   **9.109**
other history detectives say Booth was not killed
but made a successful escape to freedom) the
diary was discovered on his body. It was turned
over to the officer in charge of the manhunt. The
diary eventually found its way to Secretary
Stanton's office after having been officially
listed as among the personal effects found on
Booth's body. Each of the pages in the diary was
counted and numbered by the officer who first
took it from the dying man on the porch of a Mr.
Garrett. The officer, when turning this over to
Stanton, called the page numbers to the
Secretary's attention. However, when the diary
was produced at the trial, thirteen sequential
pages in the middle of the "book" had been torn
out from the binding and were missing--
unaccounted for. The officer in charge of the
federal troops stated emphatically at the court
of investigation that the pages were all
accounted for when the diary was given to
Secretary Stanton. Stanton, on the other hand,   **9.91a**
insisted that the pages were torn from the diary
before being given to him. It was a case of one
man's word against another man's word. Stanton,

9.125 5.13   [20] Frederick A. Morse, "The Trial of the
Lincoln Assassination, A Probable Usurpation of
Civil Justice" (M.A. Thesis, The Graduate
School of Cornell University, 1933), pp. 65-66.

being the superior officer, convinced the court
that the pages were missing when placed in his
hands.

Why has this diary been referred to so many
times by historians? Of what importance was it?
Why did the colonel or Stanton lie about the
missing pages? According to the colonel who
claimed that he had read the diary, the missing
pages offered incriminating evidence
implicating men holding high government office
in Washington. Although no office holder was
mentioned by name, the identification of these
individuals was eagerly sought after by the
investigating officials and the court of inquiry
but to no avail. Booth, the man who wrote the
entries in the diary, was shot and killed before
he could be questioned. Some historians doubt
that the man who was shot was Booth. Throughout
the following years, historians have searched
diligently for clues leading to the identity of
the persons left nameless in Booth's diary.
Was Stanton implicated?

One name that keeps coming to the attention
of historians is that of Edwin M. Stanton,
Secretary of War during Lincoln's
administration. It is the opinion of
Eisenschiml,[21] Bishop,[22] and Sandburg,[23]
who have documented the assassination, that

9.90

---

[21] Eisenschiml, <u>Lincoln Murdered,</u> pp. 434-
35.

[22] James Alonzo Bishop, <u>The Day Lincoln Was
Shot</u> (New York: Harper & Brothers, 1955), p.
257.

[23] Carl Sandburg, <u>The Prairie Years and the
War Years</u> (New York: Harcourt, Brace & Company,
1954), p. 723.

Stanton, a politically ambitious man and an
outspoken critic of the President, acted in a
very peculiar manner following the slaying. For
example, why did he keep the name of the assassin
a secret until three hours after the crime,
knowing that every minute's delay reduced the
chances for apprehending the criminal? No one has
been able to explain Stanton's motives for
withholding the name of the murderer when it was
an established fact that the culprit was John
Wilkes Booth. Very strange, indeed!

9.54
   Consider, also, how Stanton reacted to the
news brought to him by the chief of detectives,
General Lafayette C. Baker. Baker reported to
Stanton, "We have got Booth." Stanton said   5.29
nothing in return but waited a full minute in
silence and then left the room without a word.[24]
This was strange behavior for a man who should
have been overjoyed at the news that the manhunt
had been successful.

   General Baker was destined to meet up with an
untimely death several years later in
Philadelphia. A popular and responsible
periodical specializing in American military
history suggests that the chief of detectives may
have been poisoned with arsenic and sent to an
early grave. Baker left a coded message in a book,
eventually found by his heirs, that shows his
concern about his own safety.

   This coded message prepared by General Baker
shortly before his death alleges that Stanton
helped plot the murder of Lincoln.[25] Was it the

---

[24] Eisenschiml, Lincoln Murdered, p. 150.
[25] Robert H. Fowler, ed., "Was Stanton
Behind Lincoln's Murder?", Civil War Times, 3,
August-September 1961, p. 5.

ravings of a man beset by pain? Was it a man who   9.112
might have felt that he did not receive his fair
share of a reward for capturing Booth?

  Time erases evidence

    It is tragic that each passing year washes
away another bit of evidence of the murder.
Interpretations by investigators do not always
agree. In fact, the many different accounts serve
to muddle the tragedy even more than it already
is. If one wishes to judge Stanton on
circumstantial evidence, then the finger of
suspicion points heavily at him. However, this is
not the American way of determining the guilt or
innocence of individuals.

    Perhaps more would be known about the
conspirators in the killing if the son of this
great man had not destroyed many of his father's
personal papers. In 1925, a year before his
death, Robert Todd Lincoln burned some of his
father's unpublished papers in the family
fireplace. He gave as his reason that he saw no
useful way in which the evidence contained in the
letters and manuscripts could be used. He further
stated that the incident and all connected with
it were lost to time and he did not wish to reopen
the case. Robert Lincoln never elaborated upon
his comments and in so doing added more mystery to
the murder that was already cloaked in mystery.
We can only conjecture as to the contents of the
burned papers.[26]   9.115

8.30
9.47   It is almost a certainty that the motives for

9.76   [26] Emanuel Hertz, The Hidden Lincoln (New
9.115   York: The Viking Press, 1938), Preface.

killing the President, the mysteries surrounding
the event, the identity of the conspirators, and
the actions of individuals close to the President
9.47   will never be fully known.

9.46

9.137

9.135

9.138

BIBLIOGRAPHY

9.45

9.139   Bishop, James Alonzo. <u>The Day Lincoln Was Shot</u>.
             New York: Harper & Brothers, 1955.

         Current, Richard N. <u>Mr. Lincoln</u>. New York: Dodd,
             Mead and Co., 1957.

9.140
5.6   Eisenschiml, Otto. <u>Why Was Lincoln Murdered?</u>
             New York: Grosset and Dunlap, 1937.
9.141

         Fowler, Robert H., ed., "Was Stanton Behind   9.102
             Lincoln's Murder?" <u>Civil War Times</u>, 3,
             August-September 1961.

9.75   Hertz, Emanuel. <u>The Hidden Lincoln</u>. New York:
             The Viking Press, 1938.

         Kelly, Edward James. <u>The Crime at Ford's
             Theatre</u>. Washington, DC: Government
             Service, Inc., Action Publishers, 1944.

         Morse, Frederick A. "The Trial of the Lincoln
             Assassins, A Probable Usurpation of
             Civil Justice." M.A. Thesis, The
             Graduate School of Cornell University,
             Ithaca, New York, 1933.

         <u>New York Herald</u>, Saturday, April 15, 1865.

         Sandburg, Carl. <u>The Prairie Years and the War
             Years</u>. New York: Harcourt, Brace and
             Company, 1954.

         U. S. Department of the Interior. <u>Lincoln Museum
             and the House Where Lincoln Died</u>.
             Booklet, reprint. Washington, DC:
             Government Printing Office, 1956.

         <u>World Book Encyclopedia</u>, 1982 ed. S.v.
             "Lincoln."

Appendix C

TERM PAPER CHECKLIST

Chapter Reference		Yes	No
8.4.	1. Does my introductory paragraph get the paper off to a flying start?	____	____
C 1, p. 4.	2. Does the introductory section state specifically the purpose of my paper?	____	____
7.5, 8.12.	3. Have I developed the body of the paper according to the outline?	____	____
8.32.	4. Does each paragraph link up with the previous and following paragraphs?	____	____
8.28.	5. Does each paragraph have one central thought?	____	____
8.28.	6. Does each paragraph have a good opening sentence such as a topic sentence?	____	____
8.28.	7. Does the remainder of the paragraph relate to the beginning topic sentence?	____	____
C 1, p. 4, 7.8.	8. Does the paper accomplish my objective as stated in the opening paragraph?	____	____
C 1, p. 4.	9. Do my conclusions rest on the evidence presented in the paper?	____	____
8.32.	10. Have I been consistent in my use of present, past, and/or future tense?	____	____
8.32.	11. Have I decided which tense is most appropriate for my paper?	____	____
C 1, p. 4.	12. Do all comments of my own stem from my findings?	____	____
8.32.	13. As I read the paper, is it clear and does it make sense?	____	____

continued on next page

Chapter Reference		*Yes*	*No*
C 1, p. 4, 8.9, 11.34, .36	14. Have I used specific and concrete action verbs rather than weak and unclear passive ones?	___	___
C 1, p. 4, 11.38.	15. Have I refrained from overusing words and phrases that can easily be replaced with other choices of expression?	___	___
8.10.	16. Have I minimized personal references by not using words such as I, we?	___	___
8.37, 11.40.	17. Does the language sound like me?	___	___
C 1, p. 2, C 8 Intro., 8.37.	18. Does my paper show scholarly effort?	___	___
8.34.	19. Have I eliminated meanderings and unnecessary repetitions?	___	___
8.29, 11.40.	20. Are the lengths of my sentences varied to avoid monotony?	___	___
8.22.	21. Have I refrained from drawing too much material from one source?	___	___
6.20.	22. Have I checked the accuracy of my quoted matter?	___	___
8.21, 9.133.	23. Are short quotations of three or four lines or less enclosed in quotation marks and made part of the contextual matter?	___	___
8.24, 9.130.	24. Are longer quotations indented and set off in single-spaced type without quotation marks?	___	___
8.20.	25. Does each quotation have a footnote reference?	___	___
9.134–.141.	26. Is the bibliography in correct form?	___	___
5.9.	27. Is one method of numbering footnotes used consistently throughout the paper?	___	___
8.35.	28. Have I double-checked the accuracy of the footnotes?	___	___
5.6, 8.20.	29. Is every source mentioned in a footnote included in the bibliography?	___	___

continued on next page

Chapter Reference		Yes	No
C 1, pp. 2, 4. 2.8.	30. Is the paper interesting to read?	___	___
C 1, pp. 2, 4, C 9, Intro.	31. Does the paper reflect my best effort?	___	___
Para, 9.142.	32. Is my paper's physical appearance neat and attractive?	___	___
8.8, 8.31–.32.	33. Is the paper free from grammatical errors?	___	___
2.8, 2.20.	34. Does my paper offer a new "twist" on my subject or another variation of the theme explored?	___	___
9.35–.37.	35. Are the pages, except page 1, numbered in the upper right-hand corner in the correct order?	___	___
2.2, 8.2.	36. Does my paper meet the criteria of the instructor's assignment for length, scope, and interest?	___	___
2.1.	37. Am I going to be ready to hand in my paper on the date it is due?	___	___
8.43–.47.	38. Are my tables, graphs, and charts easy to read and interpret, and are they accurate?	___	___
8.43.	39. Have I used tables and graphics to support my paper?	___	___
8.50.	40. Are my graphics neatly drawn or copied?	___	___
8.53.	41. Have I had a friend proofread and critique the paper?	___	___
8.31, 8.34.	42. Have *I* proofread the paper?	___	___
8.16, 9.17, 10.47.	43. Have I retained a copy of the paper in case the original gets lost or misplaced?	___	___

Each of the above questions should be answered with a "Yes." If you have answered with a "No," check that particular aspect of your term paper because you have done something wrong.

Appendix D

ABBREVIATIONS COMMONLY USED IN REFERENCE BOOKS

A.D.	after the birth of Christ *(Anno Domini,* in the year of our Lord)
ad loc.	at the passage cited *(ad locum,* to or at the place)
aet.	aged
anon.	anonymous
ante	before
app.	appendix
art.	article
b.	born
B.C.	before Christ
bibliog.	bibliography
bk.	book
bull.	bulletin
C. or ©	copyright
ca.	about *(circa)*
cf.	compare
cf. ante	compare above
cf. post	compare below
chap.	chapter
CIJE	Current Index to Journals in Education
col.	column
comp.	compiled, -er
Cong.	Congress
Cong. Rec.	Congressional Record
d.	died
DA	Dissertation Abstracts
D.A.	Doctor of Arts
DAI	Dissertation Abstracts International
diss.	dissertation
div.	division
ed.	edited, -or
ed. cit.	the edition cited
e.g.	for example *(exempli gratia)*

encyc.	encyclopedia
enl.	enlarged
ERIC	Educational Resources Information Center
esp.	especially
et al.	and others *(et alii)*
etc.	and so forth *(et cetera)*
et passim	here and there
et seq.	and the following *(et sequens)*
ex.	example
f.	following page
fac.	facsimile
fasc.	fascicle
ff.	and the following pages
fig.	figure
fl.	flourished, greatest development or influence
fn.	footnote
fol.	folio
front.	frontispiece
hist.	history, -ical, -ian
ibid.	in the same place *(ibidem)*
id. or idem	that same person
i.e.	that is *(id est)*
illus.	illustrated, -tion
infra.	below
in re	about
introd.	introduction, -ed
jour.	journal
l.	line
lang.	language
loc. cit.	in the place cited *(loco citato)*
MEDLARS	Medical Literature Analyze Retrieval System
MS. (MSS.)	manuscript(s)
narr.	narrated by
n.b.	note well *(nota bene)*
n.d.	no date
n.n.	no name
no publ.	no publisher
n.p.	no place given for publication
N.S.	new series (calendar)
numb.	numbered
op. cit.	in the work cited *(opere citato)*
O.S.	old series (calendar)
p.	page

par.	paragraph
passim	here and there
PC	Personal computer
per se	by itself, of itself
pl.	plate
post	after
pp.	pages
pp. 2ff.	page 2 and the following page
pref.	preface
Ps.	Psalm
pseud.	pseudonym
pt.	part
pub.	published, -ication
q.v.	which see, whom see *(quantum vis; quode vide)*
r. or recto	right-hand page of a book
RAM	random access memory
rev.	revised
RIE	Resources in Education
ROM	read-only memory
rpt	reprint, reprinted
sc.	scene
scil.	to wit *(scilicet)*
sec.	section
ser.	series
sic	thus
sig.	signature
st.	stanza
supp.	supplement
supra	above
s.v.	under the word or heading *(sub verbo)*
trans.	translated, -or, -ion
v., vide	see
v. or verso	left-hand page of a book
vide ante	see the preceding
vide infra	see below or the following
vide supra	see above
viz.	namely *(videlicet)*
vol.	volume
v.s.	see above *(vide supra)*
vs.	against

INDEX

Note: References are to paragraphs,
unless specifically otherwise stated.